repaired 4/09

BY
HORATIO W. DRESSER

Methods and Problems of Spiritual Healing.
16mo $1.00

The Power of Silence.
16mo $1.25

The Perfect Whole.
16mo $1.25

Voices of Hope.
16mo $1.25

In Search of a Soul.
16mo $1.25

The Heart of It.
16mo 75

Voices of Freedom.
16mo $1.25

Living by the Spirit
32mo . . . .

THE POWER OF SILENCE

AN INTERPRETATION OF LIFE IN ITS RELATION
TO HEALTH AND HAPPINESS

BY

HORATIO W. DRESSER

"Ye taught my lips a single speech
And a thousand silences"
EMERSON

TENTH EDITION

G. P. PUTNAM'S SONS
NEW YORK & LONDON
The Knickerbocker Press
1900

Copyright, 1895
BY
HORATIO W. DRESSER

To my Father and Mother,

JULIUS A. DRESSER,
ANNETTA G. DRESSER,

THIS VOLUME IS GRATEFULLY INSCRIBED.

PREFACE TO FOURTH EDITION.

THE essays published in this volume were read as lectures to small audiences in Boston during the season of 1893-94. Chapter II., "The Immanent God," was then issued in pamphlet form; and its cordial reception led to the revision and publication of the remaining papers in the series. The sale of the book has been most unexpected since its appearance in May, 1895. It has won its way, and appealed to those whom the author had no thought of reaching when he published it. Of these some have read it because its doctrine of the immanent Spirit interpreted their own deepest convictions. Others have found it acceptable so far as its theory is concerned, but have been unable to accept its application to health. Still another class have criticised it because of its silence in regard to the Christ. That it in no way aims to be a "substitute" for Christianity, but is thoroughly in harmony with the spirit of Jesus' teaching, surely no one can question who reads it sympathetically. So far as it advocates the new philosophy of health, it is based upon actual observation of just such practice in the care of the sick as it advises for all who are willing faithfully to apply its teaching. This line of thought originated more than a half-century ago in the researches of Dr. P. P. Quimby, of Belfast, Me., who devoted **twenty-five years** to its application and development.

With him the author's father and mother were for some time associated previous to his death in 1866; and without their long experience and teaching, of particular value in Chapters V. and VIII., this book would have been impossible. Nevertheless, the book is a sincere confession of the author's own experience in the search for truth. It aims to speak from soul to soul, to make vital in every moment of experience the sustaining presence of the Spirit. As such, it is offered fully as much for its philosophical as for its practical value. This phase of it has been somewhat neglected in the eagerness to accept or condemn its theory of health, while some have found it pantheistic and mystical. In a recently published book, entitled "The Perfect Whole," dealing more especially with ethical and metaphysical questions, the author has endeavored to meet these objections, and to develop the doctrine of the unity of all things in one fundamental Spirit far more systematically than was possible in this volume. But the book has already found its place by the operation of that spiritual affinity which draws kindred souls together. If it shall continue to be helpful to those who seek daily light in the boundless realms of the soul, its further mission will be far greater as a clue to the Spirit than as a discussion of the more technical problems of philosophy.

H. W. D.

19 BLAGDEN STREET, BOSTON, MASS.
October 1, 1896.

CONTENTS.

CHAPTER		PAGE
I.	Introductory	9
II.	The Immanent God	17
III.	The World of Manifestation	48
IV.	Our Life in Mind	71
V.	The Meaning of Suffering	104
VI.	Adjustment to Life	131
VII.	Poise	161
VIII.	Self-help	191

I.

INTRODUCTORY.

ONE characteristic stands out above all others in the century of thought now rapidly drawing to a close. It is an age of persistent and unsparing inquiry, of search for causes, sources, origins. It is not content with faith alone, but seeks reasons. The distinctions between schools and systems of thought are fading out in the light of the larger sympathy and sense of brotherhood which the age inspires. The ideal of a universal human society, a universal science, and a universal religion, is already dawning upon us. Students of history, of nature, of human thought and society, are endeavoring to draw an accurate picture of the world-life of the past out of which the present has necessarily proceeded. There is a new demand made upon man,—to understand himself in the light of all the causes that have operated to produce him, his thought, his daily experience, his joy and suffering. This desire to know the origin of beings and things as a progressing whole gives the clue to the method and purpose of the present volume.

Its first object is to be helpful, but not in the traditional way. It urges no mere acceptance of its doctrine, proposes no name for its theory, and claims neither originality nor finality for its teaching. It offers reasons for certain phases of the inner life which have hitherto remained mysterious. It is offered as a possible stimulus to systematic and patient inquiry. But it has a far deeper object than this, a purpose in which it will fail unless it be perfectly clear from the outset that this volume is something more than a restatement of the great and beautiful truths which were enunciated so long ago.

This purpose will become apparent by considering the difference between one person and another. Life is a problem which has for each an individual solution. No one can wholly solve it for us or take from it the element of personal responsibility. It has its own particular history and meaning in each individual case. Difference in temperament and in experience gives infinite variety to these personal solutions. The utmost that one individual can do for another is to enunciate the principles which underlie all experiences, however varied. Truth is not truth for us until we have made it our own through reflection, until we have applied it in daily life.

It is hoped, then, that the reader will stop at every important point, as the discussion approaches daily life, to make the thought his own through quiet realization of its spirit and its meaning. Let him pause in restful silence to ask, without forcing himself to think, What does this mean for me? How does it explain, how does it accord with my experience? Have I ever devoted time and reflection — alone with my deepest self — to realize the full bearing of the profoundest and sublimest truths of life? Have I ever made them my own and actualized them in daily life, or is there still a chasm between theory and practice?

If the reader will keep this practical object constantly in view, unsuspected applications of well-known truths will become apparent before the volume is finished.

This book does not, however, advise rigorous self-analysis of the personal self alone. It seeks a way of escape from narrowing introspection and self-consciousness. It seeks the Origin of all consciousness and all life. It proceeds on the principle that man cannot fully understand himself without constant reference to the omnipresent Spirit in whom he lives, and that in this profoundest wisdom is to be found the one unfailing resource in every moment of need. It is not an inquiry alone. It is a chapter from life, an appeal to life, and aims to give the thing itself, so far as possible, instead of talking about it. The principles on which it insists are the outgrowth of experience emphasized by reason. It therefore appeals both to the reason of the reader and to those deeper feelings which find their reason in our relationship to the great Over-Soul. How else can one hope to unite philosophy and life?

It is obviously better to be true to all aspects of life as it appears from the angle of one's own temperament and experience than to force all facts into a particular system. The deepest facts are usually slighted, if not excluded, by the latter process. No formula seems large enough to cover all we know and feel. There is an element in experience that always eludes us. Some experiences can never be told. They are part of us. They are sacred, and one hesitates to speak of them. Yet one can suggest them, or at least let it be known that in these rarest moments of existence one seemed most truly to live. Only in this way does the soul, or that part of us which is most truly individual, find partial expression in language. Only in this way does the unfettered soul show its freedom from prejudice and dogma. Allegiance to a person or theory limits one to the particular view of life represented by that person or theory. To claim finality for one's system of thought would be equivalent to affirming that progress shall end with that particular discussion. Our theories serve us well so long as we remember that life itself is larger.

Life, then, is large, and demands a broad way of thinking about it. To the majority, it is true, life is a mystery into which it is futile to delve too deeply, or it is a series of experiences at once so contradictory and fragmentary that no one can deduce any meaning from them. We have no sense of what our total self means. We suffer, and we seek relief. We are absorbed in the present, in its needs and woes, unaware that our whole past lives, our inheritance and our temperament, may affect this bit of suffering nature which for the moment limits our thought. Thus experience everywhere lacks perspective. Our thinking is painfully narrow. We do not look far enough. We live as though time were soon to cease, and prudence would not permit us an hour for quiet reflection.

Yet a new phase, and to some the happiest phase, of life begins when we become conscious of our intimate relation to eternity, when we stop hurried thought, and try quietly to realize what life means as a progressing whole. If life be one, and reveal one purpose, one God, can any other interpretation be rational, will the parts ever assume their true relationship in our minds except when viewed in the light of the whole? If all power be one, and resident in the universe, acting through something or somebody, can we not discover how it is acting, and thereby learn the course of events as related to our own lives? Can we not become adjusted to the situation as it actually is, and stop this continual rebellion, this sense of dis-ease and lack of harmony with the inevitable? Possibly our suffering is largely unnecessary, and is caused by our own attitude. Possibly, too, it has a deeper meaning than we had suspected.

But before we can bring about a change of attitude, before we can realize the power of silence, we must have a firm basis to stand upon, we must know what that power is. The presence of an unwordable element in our deepest experience is no excuse for vagueness. The thoughtful mind of to-day is no longer content with mere scepticism or with mere unproved assertion. We must have a reason for our faith: otherwise it is no faith at all, and the first trying experience will set us once more adrift at the mercy of fear and opinion.

Finally, then, this book aims to be positive and hopeful, in spirit and in teaching. Its first proposition is: —

Experience is best explained by its immediate environment. The truth is involved in the very nature of the beings and things by which we are surrounded. It only needs to be evolved or made explicit. All power is immanent. It works through something. Man should not look beyond his own nature, his own temperament, inheritance, education, until he is compelled to do so in order to find an adequate explanation of his experience. He should have a clear conception of the closely related events out of which his own life has proceeded as an inevitable consequence, just as the river is enlarged and shaped in its course by its tributaries and the country through which it flows, yet never rises higher than its source. In a word, he must know his origin, both immediate and remote. He must start with his own personal experience, but should not stop until he have traced it to the very Source beyond which thought can never go.

This inquiry leads us to a consideration of the subject of subjects, on which one most of all hesitates to speak,— the nature and life of God. In pursuing this inquiry, the aim will be to use simple, untechnical language, with no historical references and as little dry reasoning as possible. Although this method is open to adverse criticism, it unquestionably serves the purpose of the book, namely, to deal directly with the thing itself out of which grow both philosophy and life. Truth is a sphere into which we must break somewhere. If our inquiry lead us finally to the Reality itself, we shall feel it and know it, and lay little stress on the mere words and forms that led us to the Spirit beneath them. Let us, then, make the start in some well-known fact of existence, which shall lead as quickly as possible to that on which all existence depends.

II.

THE IMMANENT GOD.

Some knowledge of the law of cause and effect lies at the basis of all systematic reflection. When a message is flashed over the wires from town to town, or the electric car transports us quickly and easily through the city streets, we know beyond all question that some cause has produced the effect which serves us so readily. The ease and rapidity with which the effect results do not deceive us. We may know little about the force in question; but we know that it acts in unvarying accordance with certain laws, the understanding of which enables us to control it. We learn further that every cause has its antecedent. The electricity is generated with energy derived ultimately from the sun. The motion of the ship, as it sails before the wind, is likewise traceable from wind to sun, from the sun to the very primal source of the motion which caused our universe to be. And we stop here only because we know not the antecedent of this first activity.

The chain of related causes and their subsequent effects is in reality endless. Without a cause nothing can happen, nothing ever happened; and with an eternally active cause in the world something must always happen. Every cause, every effect, every event in the history of the universe and in our own lives, is inseparably connected with this infinite series, extending far backward into the irrevocable past, and potentially related to an ever-dawning future. If we start with the simple motion of the hand, or the reflex nerve-action which preceded it, and seek its cause, we inevitably end with this untraceable series of closely related events, which bewilders the thought by its vastness.

What does all this signify? When did cause and effect begin? An absolute beginning is simply unthinkable. One all-embracing series of causes and effects must have existed eternally, of which our world and its activity is a part, and of which all future activity will be an outgrowth. Furthermore, if the motion of my arm is related causally to the activity of my whole body, to my brain, to my physical and mental environment, to my parents and to thousands of others who have thought and acted before me, to the world, the sun,— in a word, to all activity throughout eternity,— then the substance moved is no less a part of eternity.

To grasp this thought fully, try for a moment to conceive the absence of all existences in the universe, and then imagine the creation or appearance of something or of some being in this infinite void. Such an event is utterly inconceivable, since something could not be a product of nothing, and every result must have an efficient and substantial cause. If, then, something can neither be made from nothing, nor something become non-existent, the sum total of substance must ever be the same. It can be modified, evolved, or dissolved, but must itself be eternal.

Try now to imagine a condition of things in which there should be no motion, and conceive the beginning of motion in the illimitable and perfectly inert universe which you have conjured up. Once more the attempt is futile. Absolute and universal rest, like a perfect void, is inconceivable. Something moving would be needed wherewith to start motion, just as something substantial must have existed before a new product could result. If only one particle moved, then something moving must have caused its motion; and, if it moved once only, all existing particles would be set in motion, since all particles are causally correlated. Motion could not cease, since only a moving power could stop it, and there would be no power to stop this inhibiting force.

The cessation of motion, then, like its inception, is unthinkable. If it were not continuous, eternal, it could never have become a fact. Moreover, motion implies not only a continuous, all-embracing series of causes and effects, but the existence of the eternally moving substance already postulated. Motion also means change from place to place, from one condition to another. Change in turn implies the experience of rhythm or interval in motion, which we call time. Change also implies the experience of space, or the extension in three directions of that which is moved. Thus an eternally existing substance, uncreated and never-ceasing motion, infinite time and infinite space, are inseparably connected. Any particular substance, motion, interval, or space must be part of a great unitary whole which includes yet transcends them all. There is cause and effect, duration between them, extension of that which is moved or affected, eternal motion, and an ever-moving something whose infinite activity is thus characterized. Out of these we have constructed the universe in imagination, and this grand result is implied in the simple statement that every effect has a cause.

And what does this reasoning further signify? That there is one, and only one, eternal, omnipresent Reality, whence came all that ever existed, or ever will exist, which includes and is all that ever proceeds from it, the one, ultimate, all-embracing Cause, which needs no farther explanation. It is self-existent, uncreated, indestructible, at once the basis and the essence of all being, the one source to which all activity is ultimately traceable. It is simply Reality,— that for which we need seek no proof, since we are compelled to assume it in the very reasoning whereby we hope to prove its existence. It simply is, its own best reason for being. It is substance and power; it is life and consciousness itself, the knowledge of the existence of which is the one surest possession of human intelligence. It is, if you will, the infinite Spirit, the eternal Father, the unseen and permanent basis of the visible and transient series of causes and effects which constitute world-experience and human life. It is the great Whole, to which there is no space and no time, no beginning and no ending, whose activity is continuous, and whose substance is all there is, to which we are ultimately led if we pursue our reasoning to its last conclusion.

Were we to conceive the existence of a vast number of causes in place of the one Reality, these causes would still be correlated; they could not be independent, since every cause is the resultant of some antecedent cause, and no reality could be independent but the all-inclusive origin of which we are speaking. The last cause, could we conceive an end to the infinite chain, would still be a unit, uncreated and eternal, and would therefore be the sum total of all that ever could exist. Otherwise stated, if there were more than one reality, then these other realities would possess activity and substance revealed in space and time. No one of these realities would be omnipresent, independent, or self-existent. There would still exist an all-uniting, omnipresent Reality which would be the life and substance of all others and superior to all limitations of space and time. For the origin, being the All, is therefore infinite, including yet transcending all bounds, including and revealing itself through all forms and qualities.

When, therefore, we speak of a being or substance with limitations, when we give names and assign attributes, such as "God is love," we mean some portion of this one eternal, omnipresent, all-sufficient Reality, the one substance, the one life, the sum total of all that actually exists. Could we know this one, could we define it, we should be this one. It is known to us through its infinite self-revelation as the universe. This universe of the correlated many must exist for one supreme purpose and be governed by one transcendent law. Could we state this law and define this purpose, we should once more be this one which the many reveal. We may define it as intelligence, power, love, substance. But we have not defined It, but rather a certain attribute or manifestation as we know it. We may say that we know him, meaning a personal God. But we know him only in the one phase which appeals to our finite intelligence. The Reality is still the basis of all phases, of all attributes, of all manifestations of power and form.

Again, we may deem him imperfect, and actively engaged in thinking out his mighty problems, of which this great, pulsating universe of ours is the objective representation, part by part corresponding to his thought, and our lives representing some special phase of this problem. But why, then, this definiteness of motive, revealed alike in all the kingdoms of nature, this co-operation toward an apparently preconceived end, if he is merely experimenting with us? Would not this limited being be part of a larger Self, who knew all things from eternity, and is unlimited, infinite, and utterly beyond all definition? Conceive and define him as we may, there still remains a Reality which no statement describes, which ever recedes as we seek to grasp it, but which is all we mean when we use the terms "God," "Spirit," "life," "the universe," — yet more, which we cannot deny, since we assume it before we deny it, which imbues our thought with its presence,— yes, is our thought, is the thinker, the all in all.

But I have thus far spoken of God only as the transcendent Reality which no language can define, a Reality which some dismiss as the unknowable, while others conceive it in purely mechanical terms. It follows from the foregoing that he is also immanent, that, whatever he may be as the absolute Reality, he is known in part to us as the God of our life and of our world. While, then, in one sense there can be no space and no immanency to an All, we must consider the relationship of the whole to its parts, and see how the world of manifestation of the Many proceeds necessarily from the nature of the One.

We have seen that the events of life and of the universe are causally correlated, that they are joined in an unbroken series. And, since this series of events is part of a great unit, and there is only one Reality, all activity originates within and never outside this Reality. It is impossible, then, that some man-like God should have impressed his energy upon the primeval nebulous mass, and then retired we know not where, or that he should have made the world out of nothing in six days, and then interfered with it from time to time by miraculous providences. For there is no extra-natural Deity. The sum total of substance and force does not change. And evolution, not creation, is the law of life.

The manifold changes which have brought the world to its present state, the endless working of force against force, of animal against animal, and man against man, and the ups and downs of human history, are probably just as important and require the divine presence just as much as the impulse which first brought our world into being. Either, then,— note the alternative,— God put forth his own being as the world, immanent yet transcendent, and is with it, transforming it through phenomena, as much now, in this age, in these changing times, in this room, as in the irrevocable ages of the past, or there is no God at all. For whatever exists is a part of and within the one Reality. Nature's God, the immanent God, is the only possible God. Let me repeat. Either God is revealed through the cohesive force which holds matter together, and holds the planets in their positions in space, through the love which draws man to man, and the fortunes and misfortunes which characterize his progress, through the insensible gradations by which our politics are changing and our own conflicts are making us true men and women, or there is no divine Father at all; for science tells us of no other development but that of ever-gradual and never-ceasing evolution, due to resident forces.

Life, then, all life, yours and mine, all that holds it together and links it with the eternal forces of the universe, is a continuous, divine communication. There is no separation between our own souls and that Spirit in whom, in the most literal sense, we live and move and have our being, between the world in which we live and that eternal Reality of whose substance and of whose activity it is a part. The life which sleeps in the rock, dreams in the plant, and awakens to consciousness in man, is the same, the one great life, which is revealed just as clearly in the fortuitous changes that spur us on to progress as in the exact movements of the planets. All nature reveals God. The sea, the sky, the mountains, the complex life of great cities, the simple life of the country, the admiration of the poet, the thought and feeling of all men, all nations, all books, all churches, all religions. All thinkers, all artists and lovers of the beautiful, are feeling after him. All state in their own terms, and according to their degree of intelligence, the conception of a divine Father, which I have tried to make clear as it appears to me; namely, that he is nature, yet more than nature, personal, yet more than person; on the one hand, the great unit, omnipresent force and substance whence all things and beings proceed, impersonal, infinite, unknown, transcendent, indefinable; on the other hand, relatively known, finite, immanent, personal; an intelligent power, large enough to be the author of all life, and near enough so that Jesus could name him Father, and so that we can perceive his activity in our daily lives; an omnipresent Reality, whose complete nature is revealed in the total universe, and so much as we can comprehend in our own lives; a Spirit which has no form, but which all forms reveal; a God who is unknown and unperceived in this larger and deeper sense, except by those who have thought and suffered deeply, he whom we refuse to recognize when we look afar into the heavens for a god of our own fancy; a God who is not only immanent, but is that in which he dwells,—a continuous, all-pervasive, all-pervaded Spirit; a Friend who is just as near to us in this present happy moment as in the countless æons of eternity of which this fleeting moment is an integrant part.

Do we realize what this nearness means, what it is to dwell with God consciously? Let me try to bring him yet nearer.

Sometimes one seems to look far into the eyes of a friend and to see the soul gazing from unseen depths in return; and, as the face softens into a smile, one draws still nearer to that elusive somewhat called the human spirit, as it lends life and beauty to the features, itself invisible, yet so plainly revealed that one can almost locate its vanishing touch. There are days in the country in summer — noticeably in June and September — when a divine stillness seems to rest over all the world. We feel an unwonted and indescribable peace which lifts us above our petty selves to the larger Self of eternal restfulness which nature's calm suggests. We almost worship nature at such a time, so near it brings us to the Spirit which imbues the very vibrations of the atmosphere. Again, when standing near some grand mountain, or when looking far into the clouds at sunset, we seem to perceive the strength and the vanishing glory of him who is almost revealed to our longing eyes, yet forever remains beyond our keenest vision.

And, if we push our analysis still farther, do we not discover that all that is best and dearest in human life, all that is most useful in nature, is like this retreating beauty of a soft landscape: the mechanism is visible, but the beauty is of the mind? I saw my friend, you say. Yet you only saw his face, not his soul, just as you see the world, but not the Life which animates it. You feel love, you use wisdom, you reap the inner benefits of goodness; but all is intangible. No one ever saw force: we see and make use of its effects. Yet no one doubts its existence. We know it through its manifestations. And some affirm that there is no dense material, simply varied modes of motion of one infinite force, of one underlying Reality; while other philosophers describe the universe as a system of ideas produced in us by the great Reality behind all phenomena. Whatever the ultimate nature of matter may be, and this is a question which we cannot profitably discuss here, it is evident that the Reality is somehow made known to us. No one denies it, yet no one ever saw it; so intimate is the association between motion and that which moves, between cause and effect.

The retreating beauty of nature, then, seems typical of our deepest associations with the Father, a union to which Emerson has given the best expression in his "Over-Soul." We are conscious of the human part; and, when in times of sorrow we seem comforted from on high, we are dimly aware of the divine. Yet we cannot grasp it: we can only affirm that God resides in and is the source of our being, just as the grandeur of nature resides in a landscape whose beauty we can never locate. Take love, take wisdom, start with any quality in human life which points to a common nature, and, tracing it to its source, one's thought is lost in contemplation of the great Reality which must be all these qualities, since there could be but one perfect love and wisdom, which all share in greater or lesser degree, just as surely as the force with which I move my arm is related to the power which, from all time, has caused the planets to revolve and the infinite series of causes and effects to be active.

Were we not thus a part of the one omnipresent Reality, there would then be some place where the Reality does not exist; and it would not then be omnipresent. Unless our activity is due ultimately to the one life, then there is an existence independent of it; and this we have proved impossible. Our consciousness, our life, our intelligence, must blend with the infinite life and consciousness; and this larger life must therefore be all of yet more than our own. Since this Reality is omnipresent, and is the sum total of all that exists, we must be part of it in order to exist at all, and as dependent on it as the plant on the sunlight. And, since it must be conscious in order to be aware of its own existence, it must know us as a part of itself. Thus, then, there is no escape from the conclusion that we are part of the great Reality, or God, that we reveal him when we truly love and serve and are really wise, that he knows us as a part of himself, that we have no power wholly our own, and that we do not exist apart from, but as a part of, this great Over-Soul.

In such a realization as this, that we blend in consciousness and in love with the ever-renewing Life, and that we reveal more and more of the divine nature as we ascend in the scale of being, lies a real way of escape from morbid self-interest, introspection, self-consciousness, want of confidence, and the feeling of one's own insignificance. To know that our highest love, our deepest thought, our truest self, is not wholly our own, but, in so far as it is unselfish, is divine, — this it is to have something in which we can trust and on which we can rely, which shows us what we are, not as weak human beings which we vainly try to understand by self-analysis, but what we are as particles of the divine nature. Thus the painful thought is lost in the consciousness of divine nearness, just as though a particle of sunlight should become aware of its relation to all sunlight and to the sun. And what a pleasure it is to view nature and human life with an ever-deepening consciousness of this divine background! Truly, there is no time for complaint, or even for suffering, so far as suffering is self-caused, if we dwell in this pure region of thought, where we look upon the good and true as an outburst of the divine, and all else as slowly evolving toward this realm of goodness, where the landscape suggests the beauty which it so well typifies, and where our own hardships lead us, not into the realm of complaint, but into the land of inquiry, of genuine desire to know what God is doing with us.

But the question still remains, How can the infinite become finite? How can a perfect God know imperfect man, with all his woes and struggles? Why should he create? The answer is contained in what we have already said concerning the one Reality.

Continuity of motion is one of the attributes of that Reality, the activity of which originates within itself, and is never self-destructive. Eternal self-interaction is the cause of eternal self-manifestation. The Reality has therefore never been without manifestation. Although it is the One, it must ever have been the Many: it must ever have been at once finite and infinite, since it is not simply an undivided whole, but is the sum of all its parts, each one of which, like the figures 1, 2, 3, is finite. Motion could not spring suddenly out of a perfectly simple, inert unit. Even an ultimate cause must be substantial and active from eternity, and have something on which to act. We need not then try to conceive the beginning of this universe, for it never had a beginning except in its transitory aspects. Nor need we conceive a motive for the first manifestation of the one Reality, since it could not exist without manifestation; and whatever appears is at once a part of itself and an outgrowth of that which has actively existed throughout eternity.

The One is the sum total of all possibilities: it is eternally the Many, either actually or potentially. If it be actually the Many, then there is always somewhere all possible forms of manifestation. If the One be only potentially the Many, then we are bound to conceive it as progressively manifested in a world-order like our own, and must expect a continuance of the series until the whole has been expressed in finite form. The One, then, must ever have been perfect in every possible sense of the word, but only perfect through its transcendent unifying of the Many, either immediately or progressively making itself known to itself, and thereby giving the One an eternal object.

Put in more familiar phraseology, Could a perfect being exist without some object of his love and wisdom, without some manifestation whereby he should know himself? And, if God is perfect intelligence, does he not know all possibilities, both of divine and of human action? Is he not present in the very struggles and conflicts which we try so hard to reconcile with his unfailing love?

Unless some change take place, even in a perfect universe there could be no object of divine knowledge; and, if a change take place, there must be some consciousness of it. Furthermore, an infinite being would at least have a desire to know itself, to vary its pure monotonous self-consciousness; and, unless it had such a desire, it could never become perfect, since it must want to know itself not only through its foreseeing intuition, but through the realization of its own foresight, through self-experience and manifestation of all its attributes.

The infinite Self, or God, must, then, have thought and desire, or some form of consciousness transcending what we denote by these words. He must reveal and know himself part by part, as the finite, as the world, as man, in human love and aspiration, in order to know his total self. For, if we have come into being unnecessarily, then some other god rules, and not the all-wise Father in whom we believe, and who seems to need us. The very effort to be rational, the act of self-knowledge, consists in separating off some portion of the infinite in such manner that it shall represent a phase of the total life. And are we not just such differing aspects of a common nature, with our varied temperaments and our diverse ideas?

Since, then, the infinitely self-conscious Reality includes within itself all possibilities of thought and action, before its boundless contemplation must pass all that could ever be thought. God must see the outcome of all these thoughts, were they to be objectified in outer life, with all the suffering involved, and then chooses, if we admit the possibility that our world-order might have differed from the present system, and fixes upon the system which he proceeds to realize. He must, then, know of our petty lives and our suffering, our longings and what they mean, or else we are greater than the cause that produced us. He must have all intelligence, all power, since whatever exists, that is he. He must surely have chosen the world-order which should most fully reveal his wish and nature; and, if that nature is one of perfect and unchanging wisdom and unending love, it follows that the universe was brought forth in love, and that it is the best possible world-order. It follows, also, that this plan of manifestation cannot be altered, since it reveals the nature of the only Reality that could ever exist, since nothing could change that Reality, and since it possessed and put all wisdom into a plan which otherwise would have defeated its object. There must, then, be a will or purpose in this world-order. For, if it had no purpose, it was called forth by a non-intelligent reality, it is simply mechanical, evolution has no deep meaning, our desire for reasons is without a basis, and there is no reality which includes our intelligence, and we have misinterpreted nature when we deemed it the product of intelligence.

In order, then, to grasp this wholeness of relationship of the great world-order, let us once more adopt the imperfect figures of human speech, and conceive this Reality as an infinitely wise, an all-loving, all-containing, all-animating Thinker, in whose comprehension the shining worlds of space and the tiniest atoms whereof matter is made are grouped in one transcendently perfect system of self-realization; through whose measured reflection are evolved planets such as our own, unvarying in their law because he is unchangeable, requiring ages of time because his reflection is measured and sure, definite in shape and known to us as matter because his purpose is rational, and because reason consists in establishing bounds, and through whose tender care we are led onward to conscious union in thought and deed with his purpose for us. Our earth, then, is a part of the great rational life of God. It has its definite orbit and a definite history; it follows unchanging laws just because it is part of a thoroughly rational life. It is distinct from other spheres of the infinite activity, just because its history fulfils a purpose, and is therefore moral. It is finite, because it is a part only of this morally rational life. And so, let me repeat, with you and me. We are expressions of the infinite life, yet are finite just because the all-seeing intelligence means one thing in your life, and something else in mine. We are imperfect, incomplete, because we join with others to form his meaning; and he has not yet reflected our lives to their perfect conclusion, — a process which we are confident he will complete, though it take eternity.

Such a figure as this, the relation of a thinker to his progressive system of thoughts, seems most nearly to approximate the nearness which human speech can barely suggest. I am trying to show that God knows us, even though we fail to know him, that he has a purpose with us which he is even now executing, that he is the completing Self without which our lives have little meaning, the knower and the known, the thinker and the thoughts, the builder and the built, the sustainer and the love which sustains, the limiter whose will we know as fate and as matter, without whom we are as naught, with whom as gods.

In those rarest moments of human life when the soul, in the peaceful isolation of the woods, by the sea, or in the quiet of the library, is lifted above itself and made aware of its kinship with the Father, have you not been conscious of just such relationship as this? Has not God seemed for the moment to belong to you alone, as though in the unsearchable depth of his love he lived for you? Yet were you not conscious that the Spirit which then moved you to silence is the same which speaks throughout the countless spheres of the universe? What a divine joy would life be could we always maintain this consciousness of the inner presence! But are we not apt to forget this nearness, to fear, to worry, and to act as though we were independent of the great Reality, the all-seeing Father, without whom we could not be?

The present paper is simply an attempt to lend system to these rare moments of uplifting, that we may become more conscious of the divine inflow. And what is life for, in the deepest sense, if it be not to bring us to consciousness of its source and its import? Is it not in our moments of earnest thought, when we reflect on experience and learn its meaning, that we grow? And, if mankind were judged on the basis of real worth, would not so much avail as we really are as thinking, helpful souls,—that part of us which, as we hope, survives all change?

Man may be called a point of energy, a centre of application of divine Power. His consciousness, his will, if he be aware of his eternal birthright, is a vantage-point whence the infinite Thinker views the world and thereby knows himself. But the infinite Self seems to act through the majority of men almost by force, for they seem unaware of his presence. They are moved in throngs, and spurred along by suffering, because in their shortsightedness they fear and oppose the moving which is for their deepest good. As Emerson puts it, "We are used as brute atoms until we think, then we use all the rest." Yet, if this world-order is the best possible order, the love of God must be just as clearly manifested in the struggles which carry us along until we think as in our moments of repose. It is character that avails, that seems to be the purpose of our contests; and character is the result of determined effort to surmount the obstacles we are compelled to meet until we learn to live above our troubles. The experiences of evil and suffering seem justified by their outcome, since we should know nothing without experience.

Without contrast and comparison we could not interpret experience. Without darkness and evil we should not know light and good, even if we were perfect at the start, since our perfection, like that of a God without manifestation, would simply be an unrealized ideal. It is the one who has lived and suffered, conquered, thought, and practised his own truest wisdom, who moves with fate. He is no longer as one among thousands, but himself a mover, a sharer of power, co-operating in intelligent companionship with the Father. Then dawns the Christ-consciousness, with its accompanying life of self-sacrifice; and the faithful soul enjoys a personal relationship with God, whom he now knows through actual experience to be literally the All.

But our realization of the immanence of God must do more for us than simply to furnish a rational and intuitive basis for belief in an omnipresent Reality. A lasting benefit and mental freedom come from systematic thinking about life, as well as a measure of inner repose when we have pushed through doubt to settled conviction. But the real test of faith comes in moments of trouble and periods of discouragement and sickness. If we say that we believe in God, and then worry, doubt, and fear, and return to our selfish life, then we do not yet know the omnipresent Comforter. To act as though we really believed that God is in his world, in our own souls, concerned in our daily experiences, and ready to strengthen us in any need whatsoever,— this is a genuine test of faith. To lift our thoughts to him habitually, not periodically, as if we really expected to get health and help from him, instead of asking for the impossible,— this is genuine prayer.

Do we put our faith to such a test? Do we try to trust God fully, understandingly, with a deep conviction that it is his life, his power, that is pressing upon us through what we call the remedial forces of nature, through the very life of the body? Do we wait for guidance when we are perplexed? Do we try to see the divine meaning, the outcome of our experience as an integrant part of a great world-experience? Do we let this life come as it may from the divine source, without rebellion, without doubt, carrying before us an ever-renewed ideal of ourselves as happy, useful, in good health, every day in our experience having some meaning in the divine economy? Do we turn from matter to the Reality behind it; from the body to the soul that moulds it, now in this fashion, now in that, by the power of thought; from the ills which seem so real while we dwell upon them to the inner self which can become so strong that we shall have no ills whatever except those which are essential to our truest evolution?

I am not asking these questions from the point of view of some ideal theory. There are earnest souls who make this practical realization of the immanence of God the basis of a system of healing at once removed from all formulas of suggestion, assertion, denial, and from all methods of physical cure. To such the overwhelming power which accompanies this realization and the desire to help the sufferer is everlasting evidence of its truth. And all hypnotic processes would be as superfluous as they would be irreverent in the presence of this divine power, alike inspiring humility and confidence in its renewing strength.

Nor am I advocating mere religious faith in God, or an easy-going optimism which assures us that somehow all will come out well. I am pleading, first, for a scientific interpretation of the world; secondly, for a conception of an underlying Reality, an indwelling Spirit, large enough to give continuous life to this world; and, finally, for wise adjustment to and intelligent co-operation with the impulses which spring from this indwelling life. I advocate that interpretation of life which places the responsibility largely on ourselves, which teaches us not to lean on systems of thought and on people in whom we believe and whom we permit to do our thinking for us, but encourages us to look within and to find in our own souls an ever-present resource.

Deep within every human soul there is a dormant intuition which, if it be quickened, will guide us, as unerringly as the instinct of the dove, to our centre, to our home in God. There are those who, aware of this divine instinct, await its word and rely on its guidance with just as much assurance as the most ardent believers in science await her profound conclusions. They make almost no plans, but look upon the task which comes to them to do as bearing some relation to the great life of the All. Their faith is based on accurate and long-continued observation of the phenomena of the inner life, on oft-repeated proof that help and guidance are ready for those who listen confidently and receptively. Is there not a possibility here, an ever-present yet universally neglected resource, capable of bringing such usefulness and joy into existence as we have never dreamed of?

It seems unbusinesslike to await impressions, to trust. Yet the merest reflection proves that all life reposes on trust. The reputation of a business house can be ruined in an hour, if its standing be seriously questioned and the report be noised about. With all that science has told us about nature's laws, we are still compelled to take the world on trust. We fall quietly asleep at night, believing that the day will dawn tomorrow, that no calamity will befall our world, that it will be safe to depend on nature's forces. Nature has never deceived us, and we believe she never will. Yet we do not know what may happen. We run a thousand risks each day, in the streets, in the cars, everywhere, with perfect composure. Can we not carry our trust a bit farther and understand that on which we should rely, and not only rely upon it, but call upon it for aid? Is God less watchful, is he any less present in the realm where thought controls and leads us into fear and dis-ease or into trust and composure, according to our direction of mind? If gravitation holds the earth in its position in space, may it not be that its spiritual counterpart, the love of God, sustains our souls in their progress, and provides for us in ways which we have scarcely suspected? Yet how many of those who say, God is love, stop to realize the world of meaning in that little sentence? There is healing and comfort in such realization. Let me suggest it briefly in closing.

The omnipresent Reality, or immanent God, must love the world he has brought forth to reveal him, and therefore must appreciate and love you and me as parts of it. He must have caused it to evolve from love or desire, for otherwise he would have been compelled to cause its existence. Had he been compelled against his will, the existence of a compeller would be implied; and this is impossible, since there is but one Reality. Since he is the All, he is all the love there is; and, since he must of necessity reveal himself in order to have an object of his inexpressible devotion, he must have put himself forth in love. And, if he brought us here in love, he must care for our continued welfare, since he is unchangeable. If he cares for us, he must have had a loving purpose in causing us to exist; for he was not compelled to bring us into being. He is all-wise, and could not have brought us here without knowing his own purpose. No one can defeat his purpose since he alone exists. His purpose cannot be self-destructive, nor can he wish us harm, since he called us forth in love. If he loves us, he must be with us, since a distant God is impossible, and would be cold and unfeeling, while the true God is our larger, our diviner self, nearer to us than thought, closer than thought can imagine. His relation to us must ever be intimate, since there is no power, no substance, no space, to separate us. Therefore we are not in any sense apart from him. We exist with him in a relationship typified by that of a child in its mother's arms. He is our Father, though infinite in power and wisdom. Nothing can prevent us from enjoying his love, his help, his peace, his inspiring guidance, but our own failure to recognize his presence. Let us, then, be still and know his love, his indwelling presence. Let us test it fully, and learn what it will do for us if we never worry, never fear, never reach out and away from this present life. Let us absorb from his love as the plant absorbs from the sunlight; for our spirits, like the plants, need daily nourishment.

Can we estimate the value of such quieting reflection as this, if it be renewed day by day? Sometimes a text of Scripture, a poem, or a piece of soft music, will bring it to us. Sometimes we must seek the solitude of nature ere the Spirit come; for it is the Spirit that is the essential, and not, I insist, any form of words, or assertions, or suggestions. Silently and unobserved, the Spirit will breathe upon us if we reflect, if we wait for it in stillness day by day. It will not come if we doubt, if we fear, or — note this especially — if our own thought be too active; for the Spirit never intrudes. It lets us go our own way if we choose: it comes, we know not how, if we trust. All it asks is receptive listening. Then all an unselfish human being would wisely ask is ours.

It steals into our consciousness when we think deeply, to guide, to strengthen, to heal, to encourage. The great secret of life is to know how, in our own way, to be receptive to it, how to read the message of its inner whispering. The sure method of growing strong in realization of its nearness is to believe it will come if we listen, to trust it in moments of doubt as the lost hunter trusts his horse in the forest, to have an ideal outlook, and then renew our realization day by day, ever remembering that, as this Spirit is the only Reality, the one power, the one love, we live in it, and with it, and there is naught to separate us from its ever-watchful care, its ever-loving presence.

III.

THE WORLD OF MANIFESTATION.

ONE grand truth is evident at every point in the foregoing discussion: Every atom, every event, every soul in the universe, is imbued with the immanent Presence; and life is a constant sharing of its power. Whatever be the starting-point in our interpretation of experience, whether in some truth of human reason, some cherished insight of the inner life, or in some simple fact of the outer world, there is no logical stopping-place short of absolute certainty that God exists as the one all-inclusive, omnipresent Reality. We may evade the point or deviate into agnosticism, through undue regard to the limitations of finite consciousness; but our own deepest nature is never satisfied until we make the escape into the Universal. Once free, the conclusion seems a necessity of thought, at once satisfactory, convincing, and unanswerable. It holds true for all time. It is the property of all who think, and lies latent in every fact of life, suggesting a wonderful broadening and deepening of human experience when this one greatest truth shall become a permanent factor in our daily thought.

The temptation is strong to turn at once to a consideration of that daily thought, and to ask, What is man? But, if we are to understand man in the light of his entire origin, we must still continue to study him in relation to his environment. Mental states are more apt to be deceptive than physical. One is inclined to read too much in them, and to draw erroneous conclusions. If we are to conceive the inner life in accurate terms, we must take our start far within the limits of the well-known outer world. We shall then have a firm basis on which to rest the more important superstructure. And, if we keep the realization of God's immanence ever before us, the discussion will not seem dry. We have already found it convenient to make certain distinctions in order to add intelligibility and vividness to our conception of God, and the beauty of the conception which thus grew upon us was its inclusiveness. We lost no deeply cherished conviction in thinking of him as the one omnipresent Reality. We shall only add to our deepening knowledge of him in considering him as the basis of his own well-ordered world of manifestation, if we remember that every part of it is instinct with his life.

We have concluded that in the nature of God

as the only Reality lies the necessary reason for the existence of our world and of our individual selves; for he must be infinitely self-conscious, he must have self-expression, in order to have an object for that boundless love which we believe him to possess. He is therefore both subject and object, both the knower and the known, the transcendent Whole, the immanent Life made known through the parts, and the varied universe through which he is partly perceived.

Moreover, this double aspect of the One is repeated throughout the universe of the many; and by tracing it out we shall find a practical solution to many vital problems. The world of manifestation becomes for finite beings a universe of mind and matter, apparently dissimilar in their nature, yet in reality identical in the One in whose transcendence their unity is hidden. The relation of God to matter is therefore just as intimate as his relation to the human soul, for whatever exists is a part of and within the one Reality. We cannot, then, consistently deny the existence of matter. To make such a denial is equivalent to asserting the non-existence of the one Reality, and therefore of our sensations, since all that we experience has some cause outside ourselves; and we know our own existence only as it is related to this outer Reality. Matter surely exists. Mind exists. How they are related in consciousness we shall soon consider. But we must begin with matter as a real existence, as a part of God, imbued with his immanent life, and in no sense independent of him. The one Reality must be the basis and substance, and the only basis and substance, of all that we call matter, just as truly as it is the Life that is active in every moment and in every incident of our inmost being.

It is undeniable that the world of matter which you and I contemplate may have no external existence precisely as we perceive it. Science tells me that certain ether waves impinge on my retina, and form an image of some external object, which in turn is translated into an idea, and interpreted according to my education. Certain other rays indirectly produce ideas in your mind, and are interpreted according to your education. The outer object may be the same in both cases; but the ideas caused by it may be quite different, owing to our different states of mind. I never see exactly the same object which you contemplate, nor do either of us as minds actually see the object at all, since we know the object by means of ideas. We are unable even to dissociate the actual sensation and the perception based on a lifetime of experience and thought by which we interpret it. Nor do we hear the same sound, perceive the same colors, nor smell the same odors. But the existence of something real which causes the sensations no one can seriously question. Even an uninterpreted sensation makes us partially aware of something not ourselves. We may be scientifically aware that the sensation is in and not outside of our minds, and that we interpret it through ideas; but the object that produces the sensation is not necessarily an idea. When the hand encounters a masonry wall, we are sure of the existence of an external force which meets and effectually withstands all the pressure we are able to exert. There is no room for doubt here.

Nor can we question the existence of accurate knowledge about the outer world. The chain of causes running back into infinity with which this discussion began is such a fact of certain knowledge. We know that certain effects will be produced on us under certain conditions,—for example, putting the hand into a fire. These outer conditions are there just the same, regardless of any interpretation of ours. Our interpretation may or may not correspond to the facts and explain the relations of objects. We did not create those conditions nor arrange objects in certain relations. They are independent of all minds. There must then be certain actual relations existing between objects and external to us which cause in us our definite experiences; for instance, of the alternation of day and night, the sensations of heat and cold, the experience of cause and effect, the reign of law, and the successive conditions of evolution. But, if they are actual relations, they must be qualities of the one Reality. They must be characteristics of his world of manifestation, since nothing real can exist independent of him. If, therefore, we study them, if we study nature and natural law as expressions of the very consciousness, the very reason, the very life of God, we shall not be stopped by materialism, we shall not be weighed down by matter, but ever draw nearer and nearer to the Spirit behind it.

Matter, then, is not a mere phenomenon, any more than is the mind that partially knows it. Ultimately it is a real substance. It is part of the one enduring Reality, the cause or series of causes of the world of sense-experience. It is the real substance partially perceived and judged according to our opinions and temperament: it is the means whereby we contemplate the One. Reality is both the universe as God knows it and the God who knows it. As matter, it is his meaning, his purpose made manifest: it is God realizing himself in definite form, the tangible expression of his purpose holding man in the straight and narrow pathway of progress, the Spirit put in limited form so that we can grasp it.

But enough of the abstract. If there is now no possibility of misunderstanding the point of view of this book in regard to the existence of matter, we are ready to consider those qualities of matter the understanding of which is most essential to what follows. The full bearing of this driest part of our inquiry will not be evident until the last chapter. We shall then see how the best known facts of the outer world clarify the vaguer facts of the inner life, and reveal the secret of self-help.

Our first experiences in life are fragmentary sensations from this outer world. That the world is shrouded in manifold illusions is evident from the very outset. The infant has no sense of distance, and some people spend a lifetime without learning to judge accurately of certain distances on sea and land. There is no sense of the relation of things and events until the understanding has again and again been called into play. Thus sensation in time becomes perception, and the mind plays a part of increasing importance and value in our daily life. We strike a wall, and feel a jarring sensation. We go out into the sunlight, and feel a sense of warmth. As experience widens and our convictions become more mature, we associate these experiences, distinguish between cause and effect, and deduce from their invariable sequence a statement called a law. We affirm that, "As a man sows, so shall he reap," that nothing happens without a natural cause. Yet we are apt to forget our own generalizations; and the fact that men still sin, still cherish anger, uncharitable and unforgiving thoughts, shows that the majority of men are suffering for just this simple knowledge that action and reaction are equal, that no event happens uncaused.

Now, Science does not forget; and among her numerous generalizations there are four of particular value in our present discussion.

1. The fragmentary events of life have been reduced to a system. Nature is not a mere chaos, in which conflicting forces eternally war upon each other, but is an order, a unit, a whole, in which part is adjusted to part, like one vast mechanism. Law everywhere reigns supreme. There are no eternally warring forces, for all force is one. We think of heat, light, electricity, vital energy, as so many separate forces. Yet they can be transmuted into each other. One force revealed in varying modes of motion gives rise to all the events in the great mechanism. Science only waits to know what this

force is, in order to understand the secret of the universe.

2. In our early experience we are apt to think of matter as dead or inert. Science shows us that it is everywhere alive and nowhere inert, not even in the great rock foundations of our earth. It is probably molecular in structure: it is composed of little moving particles in a constant state of rapid vibration, and separated from each other like the stars and planets. It exists in a series of forms and substances ranging from the hard granite through less compact forms, solids, liquids, gases, and the attenuated nerve-tissues which approach the nature of mind. Furthermore, a single substance — for instance, water — passes successively through the three states of solid, liquid, and vapor, the integration and disintegration of matter in various forms being one of the most striking phenomena of material life. Even the earth's atmosphere has recently been reduced to liquid and solid forms. The chemical process called combustion is capable of liberating in an incredibly short space of time all the solid materials of a vast wooden building, and transforming them into so many invisible gases, leaving only a heap of ashes to attest the ruin. Nothing is stable in material form, nothing can resist the subtle, invisible manifestations of the one force, interpenetrating the particles

of matter, setting them into rapid vibration or causing them to appear and disappear in ever-varying combinations.

This may be illustrated by putting large shot into a receptacle until it be filled. There will still be spaces for smaller and smaller shot, then for a liquid, and finally for a gas. The chemist, starting with a liquid, — for instance, water in an air-tight jar, — and heating it to the form of steam until it fills the jar, may still repeat the process by adding alcohol, raising that to a vapor, then adding ether, and so on, showing that there are still unfilled spaces between the molecules which finer substances and forces might occupy.

The same is obviously true of the human body. We may first consider it as a unit, then as a collection of organs, an aggregation of minute cells, and a system of microscopic molecules. No bone is so dense but it may be penetrated, no space so fine between the particles that the particles may not be drawn closer together or be thrown wider apart without disturbing the unity of the body.

We are well aware of expansion and contraction due to heat and cold. The muscles become tense under the power of a sudden emotion. They are relaxed and expanded in a state of repose. In the child the muscles are moved quickly and easily, without stiffness and other restrictions, and while the muscles are active the health is generally good. In old age partial ossification takes place, and the currents of the body can no longer circulate freely. Density and contraction occur in many cases of disease; and the problem is simply to drive the particles farther apart, to break up the density, just as the block of ice is transformed into the less dense condition of water. Everywhere in nature there is expansion and contraction, due fundamentally to the driving apart or the drawing together of molecules and atoms. The radiation of the sun's energy is just such a driving apart, while the moon is cold and contracted from loss of heat. The sun's energy is once more concentrated in the form of organic life, and is taken into the body to be expanded and assimilated, but not until it has once again been put in motion by the power of heat. Heat is the medium of chemical change, and many of our misinterpreted sensations called disease are simply due to this natural expansive power breaking up some dense obstruction or inharmony in the body. A corresponding change, accompanied by a sensation of heat, takes place in the brain when for some reason considerable power is called into a certain region.

The principle is fundamental. We shall find

it of great use in the concluding chapter; for there we shall see how the subtler forces of thought act on matter, causing it to expand or contract, because it can penetrate the finest spaces. Probably the law of composition is the same in all cases; and the particles, if such exist, in the purest grade of substance are capable of penetrating any and all other substances or forces. It may be in this way that Spirit is supreme, using and revealing itself through all lower forms, making itself known to the very lowest, not by jumps, but by insensible degrees, so that there shall be no break in the divine continuity and no separation between the transcendent Spirit, its going forth as the immanent Life and its manifestation through that in which it dwells.

3. But nature is not only a law-governed unit, a mechanism animated by a single force, in which the varying substances are composed of minute particles. It is also a live organism, in which each part, each organ, pulsating with energy and instinct with life, has some meaning as related to the whole. Of this great unitary organism, throbbing with life from star to atom, man is an integrant part. He is related to it so closely that he seems in fact the central figure, whose life was prophesied from the very dawn of being. History, religion, science, literature,

present this relationship in a thousand different lights; and now a new science of sociology and ethics is taking shape in men's minds, showing that society is also an organism in which each man owes some duty to his human brotherhood.

To make this relationship perfectly clear, think for a moment what this great natural system means. In an organism no part is complete in itself, but supplements and depends on all the other parts. No part can in itself be perfect, since it would then be a separate organism. The cog-wheel may be perfectly constructed, a truly wonderful contrivance; yet it is useless unless it fit in exactly to some machine which is incomplete without it. The musical note, however pure, has no meaning for us unless it be sounded in unison with others.

The same is true of man. He cannot live in isolation. He is not good alone. He must have a particular gift or occupation, in order that perfection may at least be approximated by the whole. He is a dependent being, and in turn contributes his little share of benefit. Countless ages elapsed ere he could exist at all, and every one of the innumerable hosts that preceded him lived and struggled that he might be born. From those who labor day by day come the food, the clothing, and the homes which make continued life possible. Numberless thousands of minds have thought out and formulated that which to-day constitutes our knowledge of art, science, history, literature, and philosophy; and the largest contribution to our knowledge made by a single mind seems wonderfully small, our own original thought infinitesimally smaller. Each of these incidental forces in the worlds of nature, of society and thought, about which we think so rarely, contributes its share to the shifting series of experiences called life, each plays its part in the great organism; and there would seem to be no just system of knowledge which does not consider them all, no logical stopping-place short of universal religion, universal ethics, a deep love for and co-operation with the brotherhood of man.

4. The most important truth remains. This beautifully organized thing of life, with its wonderful law-governed parts and its co-operation of beings and things, was not made suddenly or out of hand. It has grown out of that which eternally existed. Slowly, as the seed matures in the ground and prepares the way for the bursting bud and the blooming plant, everything in nature, so far as we know, from the raising of continents to the development of man, has taken place and reached its present condition by insensible degrees. To-day is the product of yesterday, and yesterday of the day before, and so on

indefinitely. Each cause is the effect of another cause more remote. The life of the tree comes from the sun millions of miles away, but it comes through something. Its energy is stored up in the organic and inorganic materials immediately surrounding the tree, and through the heat and light transformed from the solar rays by the earth's atmosphere. The immediate environment, ancestry, and experience give rise to all living things; and all life finds its origin in a single omnipresent source. Evolution is the only law yet discovered which in any way accounts for the origin of our world. When one pauses to consider what this law is as a universal principle, it becomes evident that there could be no other.

Yet it is easy to misunderstand this principle. To many evolution simply means the derivation of man from some lost ancestor, a belief which generally arouses a feeling of repugnance; or it means that the existence of God is not necessary under this theory, and one naturally lays it aside as irreligious. Yet evolution would be of little value if it were not a universal law, just as well exemplified in the growth of the tree as in the development of new species or of a planet from a mass of nebula. It would have no ultimate meaning unless it proved the presence of God at every step in the great world process.

In the foregoing chapter we have seen that the whole problem is immensely simplified by the knowledge that all life is immanent, that the activity of beings and things is due to the power resident in that which lives and grows.

If God is immanent in one portion of the universe, he must be immanent in all. If he gives rise to a world and its people, he must be with the world in order for it to endure. This much is clear: it only remains to discover, as far as possible, the series or gradations of power and substance whereby Spirit makes itself known to and revealed as the lowest forms of being, and to note the successive stages through which all beings pass in their upward growth.

This latter task is the work of natural science; and year by year her workers are collecting evidence, classifying facts, inquiring into the causes of variation, the influence of environment, the effect of use and disuse, the transmission of acquired variations, and all other problems connected with development. Every fact makes our knowledge of the immanent God more secure. Every datum supplies a link in the infinite series of causes and effects, a series probably no less systematic than the mathematical series from one to a thousand, from a thousand to a million, in which not one figure can be omitted. Every factor plays its inevitable part. Every step bears some relation to its antecedent and its consequent. And all facts, all forces, all events, are related to the entire universe of to-day, of yesterday, of eternity. There is no break in nature's organism, but one continuous series of closely related events. There are no jumps, but only the gradual unfolding, when it is ready, of all that is involved in the budding organism.

One need only observe the social and political changes going on to-day, class contending with class and party with party, in order to discover every aspect of this universal principle. We forget this law sometimes, and undertake to force events, we endeavor to convince ourselves that there is a royal road to success; but we soon discover that we can omit no steps.

The seed planted in the ground, like the new idea sown in a wilderness of conflicting opinion, contains an indwelling principle of life, which causes it to develop along certain lines and along no others. It partakes of the soil. It grows and absorbs nutriment from the sunlight, it matures slowly, it is dependent solely on what it has within and what closely surrounds it. Its growth may be hastened within certain limits, but only by introducing a new factor. The life of the plant which it becomes in due time is a type of all evolution. It is growth, not by creation out of nothing, but through the transformation of that which already exists into something different. Its growth is due to the interaction of part on part. Its transmutation into another species can only result through the modification, the introduction into its own life of some new element. The new element once introduced, whether in the organic or the inorganic worlds, in society, in politics, in religion, a change is sure to result; and one need only await its coming.

But we have the best evidence in our own lives; and the chief problem, laying aside all discussion of particular theories of evolution, is to discover the actual course of events in daily experience, to learn how far we have gone in the upbuilding of character and soul, to aspire and to co-operate with the immanent forces of our own being.

We have an excellent example of what evolution means in the growth of our own ideas. We are born with a certain set of opinions on matters of religion, politics, and the like. There is a strong tendency toward conservatism; and we are inclined to think like our parents, and even to cherish and defend the dogmas which have come down to us. But with each experience, each new book, each new acquaintance with the world and with people, which makes an impression on us, a new factor enters into our thought; and the only way to avoid progress is to avoid contact with progressive people.

So well is this understood by certain leaders of thought that they forbid their followers to read outside of established lines; for they know that, if people think, they will change. Ideas have a resident, a stimulating life, especially when they come fresh from the minds of those to whom the world's mental progress is due. They speak to us in books. They compel our assent through reason and through people. And, once sown in the mind, they work a wonderful transformation, until they burst forth with all the power of firm conviction.

Yet the transition is ever gradual and law-governed, like the growth of the tree. No idea is established without controversy. We turn it over, weigh it, and view it in all its aspects, just as new social and political institutions grow out of controversy and long experience. The power of conviction comes only when the last objection has been met. We are involuntarily as moderate and painstaking as Nature herself. If perchance we forget the natural method, and jump at conclusions, we discover no way of making them sure but to go back and supply all the steps. If an idea appeals to us at once, it is because thought and experience have already prepared the way for its acceptance. We cannot force a full-grown idea into the mind of another any more than nature can be interfered with from without. We are compelled to seek a starting-point, to discover some idea already existing in the mind of the other person, and lead on gradually from the known to the unknown. Nor can we create a new philosophy or originate any idea which has no basis in experience. Whether we will or no, we must take cognizance of universal human knowledge, and develop our own thought from that. Psychology shows that even the wildest and most absurd fancies of the imagination are in some way products of experience.

Our own deepest self challenges us to find any possible method of growth and change except that of patient evolution, the great world-wide process of "continuous progressive change, according to unvarying laws, and by means of resident forces." * The process once called creation is as long as time itself, as wide as the universe. It is going on to-day. It will never cease until its great task be completed. It is thorough, painstaking, gradual, and sure. It is economical, careful, and direct, making use of every incident, every possible factor, every so-

* Le Conte, "Evolution and its Relation to Religious Thought," Part 1, p. 8.

called chance, so that in human life joy, sorrow, hardship, success, heredity, disposition, environment, education, society, and thought, are called into use; and all these factors have their meaning, their bearing on the ideal result. "The ideal is immanent in the real." The aspiring force speaks through the slightest incident of experience. The all-powerful, omnipresent Spirit aspires through, co-operates with, and seeks co-operation from the individual soul to whom it is ever trying to make itself known. God is immanent in evolution.

In order to make this intimate relationship of God and his world of manifestation clear and vivid, let us try for a moment to conceive the long series of forces and substances, interpenetrating and blending with each other, and descending from the central Love down through the immanent life, the higher attributes of man, the soul, the realm of mind, the physical and chemical forces, gravitation, cohesion, electricity, and the particles of matter, and all the volatile substances to the liquids, solids, and finally to the hard rock. Or, starting with the supposed nebulous mass out of which our universe grew, let us pass slowly upward through the vast cycles of cosmic time, the thought of which adds depth and meaning to the conception of God. Let us pause in silence until we feel the spirit of the ages. Good visualizers will probably call up some mental picture which suggests these vast stretches of time. Out of the gradually cooling mass which at length takes shape as our earth we shall see the dawn of life, and the moderate, patient, purposeful transition from the inorganic to the organic kingdoms, the long periods in which one form of animal life succeeded and won supremacy over another, the change from the rank vegetation of the carboniferous period to the graceful forms of to-day, the raising of continents and mountains, the retreat of the great ice-sheets which once covered large portions of the northern hemisphere, and the dim outlines of that far distant society, the herding together of men, out of which grew modern civilization.

Thus we come at last to the dawn of human history. The epochs of the past unfold before us with new meaning. We note how period has grown out of period, event out of event. Thought becomes overpowered by the vastness and complexity of civilized life in its endless phases, its manifold contributions to the arts and sciences. The great truths of religion and philosophy, the great souls of history, claim our attention at last; and thus the thought turns once more to the one Reality which this long evolutionary process suggests.

One's personal thought is lost in contemplation of the Universal. One is momentarily lifted above the present, above the world of human life, into the life of worlds, of the universe, — yes, the very life of God, of which one seems to contemplate but one of its infinite phases. One feels and knows that the human self is part of this great Life, which no words can describe. One communes with the Essence itself, the All-thing, the Spirit, the Love. Matter seems like a mere symbol as compared with this its real meaning. The Life which manifested itself so long ago in the primeval history of the earth returns to consciousness in man, and recognizes through him its own transcendent source. The soul knows the great unity henceforth, whatever be the phase of it contemplated. It habitually turns from the universe to God and from God to his great world of manifestation.

IV.

OUR LIFE IN MIND.

CERTAIN aspects of the outer world now stand out clearly before us. The universe is an order, a system, an organized whole, in which each being and thing bears some relation to all others. Everything is related, not alone through its dependence on its neighbors, but through the law of cause and effect, the one fundamental force, substance, and life, and the law by which all things come into being. The outer world seems to be composed of independent forms and hard substances. Yet all forms are transient. The dense material dissipates into invisible gases and ultimate particles; and we find nothing permanent until we turn to the realm of the invisible and persistent Power which underlies these shifting forms. Even the constant qualities of matter must have their basis in a more substantial Reality in order to be constant at all. Matter is eternal only so far as it inheres in this self-existent Reality. It is law-governed only because the One is unchangeable. And, finally, it has no satisfactory meaning for us until we view it as the very consciousness, the objectified life of God himself, of the God who is in his world, immanent in evolution and immanent in the soul.

The Reality of the outer and inner worlds, then, is one. Everything exists in God; and we, existing in him, contemplate and know his conscious manifestations, in part. We do not simply feel matter as so many distinct objects. We do not simply feel sensations of light, heat, and cold. An object, a blow, a sense of warmth, does not come directly to the soul. The object must be understood, the blow must be perceived and reported, the feeling of warmth must be translated into an idea. We feel, and also know that we feel, force or matter in some of its forms. The simple act of feeling and knowing implies the existence not only of an outer world from which our sensations come, but of a conscious being to whom that world is made known. These very words become intelligible to the reader only as they call up ideas; and back of these ideas, following one another in rapid succession in the reader's consciousness, is the reader himself contemplating, thinking over these ideas, and associating them with what reflective experience has already made clear.

Even the materialist must admit this; for, in affirming that matter alone exists, he is simply stating a product of his reason. He has put certain ideas together, and evolved them into a system. This system of ideas is to him all absorbing. It is his habitual mode of thought, and colors his entire conscious experience. As a natural consequence, he neglects one aspect of that experience. He forgets the real nature of his ideas, affirming that mind is a mere flame, a product or outgrowth of matter. But even in admitting this he surrenders the stronghold of materialism, since by his own admission this flame is conscious; and consciousness is the fundamental fact of existence. It involves all that we are, all that we know, desire, and feel, the whole universe, and the great Thinker himself.

State the case as strongly as we may for materialism, we are more certain that mind exists, for we know matter only through mind; and the materialist must account for this deepest aspect of life with all that it involves. In fact, it is futile to deny either the subjective or the objective aspects of life; for the two have evolved together. They are present in our first experience; and the infant, reaching for the picture on the distant wall, and trying to locate the objects about him, is making the first discrimination between them. He soon gets some idea of space, for he finds that he cannot reach the picture on the wall. He learns to know one person from another. He distinguishes between his body and himself; and, finally, he becomes conscious of himself as a being that can feel and will. Part of all that he sees, feels, hears, or in any way experiences is due to his understanding from the moment his discriminating consciousness is quickened. The world becomes comprehensible to him as fast as he himself develops to comprehend it. Gradually his emotions and his knowledge play a greater and greater part in his life, until he develops a personal atmosphere, which projects itself into the outer world. Impulse and imagination in time give place to reason, but the thought of the man is no less influential in its effect on his life, he is just as truly leading a life of mind; and every business transaction, every pain and pleasure, is largely dependent on the confidence or belief he puts into it.

But all this is apt to be forgotten. Man forgets that he is a soul with a body, that he is primarily a conscious being, contemplating ideas and influenced by thought. Some thought is always prominent with him. He is always devoted to something. He shapes and controls things by his thought. Yet, just because the influence of thought is constant and is a fact of the commonest experience, he is unmindful of its real power and the real nature of his life

He seems to be leading a material life, and accordingly permits himself to be overcome by that which is material. But even here it is belief which governs his conduct. As a conscious being, he could be governed by nothing else. Every act of conduct is due to a direction of mind; and the mind shapes the conduct, and draws to itself whatever corresponds to the thought, just as truly and in the same way as a magnet attracts particles of iron. As this may not be fully evident, it is well to consider the influence of thought at some length; for in this neglected factor of human experience we shall find the greatest help in the problems of health and happiness.

It is evident first of all that the impression made upon us by a given experience depends largely upon the opinion we put into it. Let a company of people of varied tastes, prejudices, and education read a thoughtful book, listen to a speaker of decided opinions, or attend an entertainment of considerable merit, and their comments will display a wonderful variety of opinion. Diametrically opposed opinions on political, religious, and philosophical questions have been maintained ever since man began to reflect. A slight or a very marked divergence of opinion separates mankind into little groups and sects the world over. Each sect offers its opinions as truth. Everywhere people accept and are influenced by opinions with surprising readiness. Thousands of people have been made miserable and thrown into a state of excitement because in their fear and ignorance they accepted the teachings of dogmatic theology about sin and a future state, to say nothing of the slavery to medical opinion and the untold suffering that has grown out of it. The credulity, the gullibility of human nature is one of its profoundest weaknesses; and I need only refer to it to suggest its bearing on our mental life. It is a guiding factor with the majority of people, and opens the door to the control of the weak by the clever, the strong, and the unprincipled. Every one is deceived at times through this inherent eagerness to believe rather than to understand, and the influence of prejudice is so subtle that only the keenest and most discerning minds are able to eliminate it to any marked degree.

We are so accustomed to obey certain ideas that we are scarcely aware of their power over us, or how true it is that "the world is what we make it." We are born with a set of ideas, born members of sects and parties in which theory, practice, and prejudice have become one. Our religion, education, and even our fears are prepared for us by other minds. Every opportunity is given us to develop along traditional lines, and it is deemed almost a blasphemy to have ideas of our own. Even if in later life one be quickened in a new direction, it is almost impossible to overcome and cast aside these deeply rooted opinions and prejudices.

We do not stop to question our beliefs. Prejudice will not permit it. People, as a rule, prefer to accept opinion without attempting to prove or disprove it. They are bored,— and it is a most lamentable fact,— they are bored by reasons and proof. It seems never to have occurred to them that man is free, and sure of his own individuality and the truth, only so far as he has gone with a rational process of thought. The tendency to think for one's self — the most helpful and healthy tendency in man — is crushed out in its infancy; and our whole system of traditional education and religion tends to shape man's belief for him. It is only when some unusually original or self-reliant thinker breaks through the hard and fast lines of rut-bound thinking that any ideas of fundamental value are given to the world. The non-sectarian and unprejudiced man of science is a very late product of evolution; and even he is prejudiced against many religious questions, and as rigorously excludes all facts that lie without the boundaries of natural science as the most bigoted conservative rules out the doctrines of the radical. The love of truth is not yet strong enough to make us seek universal truth rather than particular opinion. We think we know. Preconception blinds our eyes on every hand. We give credit to this man or this sect, as though there could be a monopoly of truth, when a little reflection would show that truth is universal, and does not hold because any man enunciates it, or because any sect champions it, but because it is inherent in the nature of things and persons.

It is a revelation to most people to discover the power of fear in their own lives. It enters into their religion. It often inspires the prejudice which stifles unbiassed inquiry. It enters into every detail of daily life. We are apprehensive, as a race. We picture calamities of every description, and dread the worst. The sensational press furnishes constant material for fear. We fear to eat this and that. We dread, anticipate, and really put ourselves in the best attitude to take certain diseases; and we live in constant fear of death. And fear is simply another form of opinion. It runs back to our willingness to believe rather than to think for ourselves. It is based on ignorance, increases in intensity with the degree of superstition, and vanishes when we understand the law of development, of cause and effect.

But the one who knows the law and obeys it without fear, the scientific man or the seer, just as truly as the savage, is building his own world from within. The world is just as large and just as intelligible as his own ability to interpret it. The artist discovers qualities in the outer world which actually do not exist for other people. He detects certain lights and shades, certain undulations of the landscape, and an endless variety of transformations during the four seasons of the year. A scientific man will discover evidences of glaciation, and read a long and most interesting history from a rock which may be a worthless obstacle to the farmer. Even the beautiful Alps were once deemed so many obstructions to travel before the love of natural scenery was developed. The same scene viewed by the novelist, the historian, the warrior, the man of business, the savage, presents just so many different aspects, depending upon their training and the class of facts which serve their purpose. It may be comical, it may be tragical, it may inspire happiness, sorrow, comfort, dread, chagrin, pity, and suggest a thousand different ideas to the beholder. All these aspects may have some basis in fact, but they are not complete pictures of the outer world. They are individual phases of it. We see things as we are.

The difference, then, is deeper than education alone. There are natural tastes, likes and dislikes, affinities and sentiments, rendering the saying "What is one man's meat is another's poison" equally applicable to the inner world. Passion colors the world according to its nature and intensity. Experiences, dispositions, theories, differ, and project themselves into every fact of life. One thinker is persistently optimistic, despite all that life brings of pain and misery; another is no less strong in his pessimism; while a third is so bigoted that he cannot be urged to take a fair view of anything, not even of his own persistently biased nature.

The very fact that the world is so large, that the one Reality is only known to us in part, or so far as experience has made it known, shows that our interpretations must differ, and that the difference is in us. Indeed, one may seriously question if the limitations of temperament will ever be overcome, if one man can ever describe life except as he sees it, modified by the general knowledge of the race. Perhaps that very feeling of individuality is fundamental in the thought of God, is the divine consciousness focalized in a given direction. If so, it is each one's duty to cultivate this profoundest individuality, and discover just what God means through it, what aspect of life one is best able to interpret.

This deeper life in mind must then take the place of the superficial world of opinion. The dogmas and influences of other people must be rigorously excluded until, in moments of silence and quiet reflection, one learns the divine point of view through the individual man.

Thus the individual thinker penetrates deeper and deeper in his analysis of our life in mind, until his consciousness seems to blend with the universal Thinker, of whose consciousness all life is a part. His means of knowing the outer world, and the influence of opinion, of prejudice, education, and temperament, prove to him that he lives in mind. But now he discovers a yet deeper reason, and once more happily makes his escape from the narrowing effects of mere self-consciousness into the greater consciousness of the Universal.

The difference between one person and another, then, is fundamental. One has only to try to put one's self in the mind of a friend in order to realize this wonderful difference. Let the friend be one's closest companion, one's mother or brother, whom one has known intimately from infancy; and even here the transition is impossible. There is something that we cannot grasp, because it is the friend's experience, and can never be ours. Personality,— what is it, whence came it, and what does it mean?

Your world and my world, how much alike, yet how utterly dissimilar! and how many and varied the aspects of a single personality as presented to different people, all equally true perhaps, all drawn out from a single source under ever-changing conditions! Self exists within self,— the social self, the self of impulse and emotion, and the self of reason, the conscious self and the subconscious, wherein we turn over and view ideas in all their aspects until they become fixed habits of thought, the fleeting ephemeral self, which reveals itself in an endless variety of moods, opinions, and feelings, and the permament self which we call soul, that deeper consciousness which blends with the Self of selves.

But some self is always uppermost. To this we are for the moment devoted, and it is this more superficial self or direction of mind that we are most concerned with in this chapter. One fact remains true of all personalities, however great the difference between them. They are all conscious beings. On the one hand come impressions from the world of matter. On the other come thoughts and influences in the sphere of mind. The two unite in consciousness, and form the world of mental life, or our interpretation of the great organized whole of which we are part. In the centre exists man. Looking one way, all that he sees is apparently material.

Looking in the other, all appears to be mind. When he seeks their unity, he finds it alone in the conscious self which underlies them both, which therefore makes his whole life mental, and which is to be explained only by reference to the one Self.

But our mental life is not made up of perceptions, emotions, and other conscious ideas alone. There is a more subtle form of thought influence than any we have yet considered. The rapid development of hypnotism has opened up a phase of this influence which throws much light on the nature of mind. The mind is even more susceptible to the power of suggestion than to the power of opinion. Opinion itself often comes in the form of suggestion, and carries a hypnotic influence with it. Indeed, the influence, the so-called magnetism, that accompanies the spoken or written word, is often more effective than a strong argument. The strong sway the weak in this way; and positive minds draw negative minds about them, which merely reflect the thought of the leader. Auto-suggestion is also a powerful factor in our mental life, and is often used, greatly to the benefit of the health. People emulate each other through unconscious suggestion. People are drawn into all sorts of fashions, fads, and influences through these silent suggestions. Every one, in fact, has some strange experience to relate nowadays, illustrative of occult influence, hidden and unsuspected communications between mind and mind, and the remarkable effect of thought upon the body in the cause and cure of disease.

Every sensitive person is also aware of mental atmospheres surrounding persons and places, just as the odor emanates from and surrounds a rose. This is especially noticeable in a church or in some great cathedral where for ages men have bowed in worship in accordance with their particular form of religion, and have left their influence behind them. Every household, town, or city has its peculiar mentality, the analysis of which reveals the characteristics of the minds that produce it. A wonderfully stimulating atmosphere pervades a great university, causing a marked change in the thought, the manners, and even the dress of the novice, who, if he be especially susceptible, is often over-stimulated by it. Wherever man has lived and thought, these atmospheres have been left behind him. They are associated with chairs where people have sat for some length of time. They are associated with clothing, and a change of clothing is therefore sufficient at times to change the state of mind. They come with books and letters sometimes revealing more of the personality that sends them forth than the person would wish. They draw people together, and cause them to think alike. There is an atmosphere about some people that warns one not to come too close, while in other cases there is instant affinity and sympathy. One occasionally meets people whose very presence is a lasting stimulus and an inspiration. One seems to take away something besides the mere memory of a noteworthy interview; and some people forget their troubles, lose their aches and pains, and are immensely benefited by simply talking with a helpful friend. Some people compel attention or obedience by their presence, and exact a surprising amount of service and homage from other people.

Character, then, is not only written in the face, expressed in conduct and language, but is sent forth as a thought atmosphere. Atmospheres impinge and leave their impressions on each other, revealing the nature, thought, and feeling of the personality which gives rise to them. This is evidently the reason why first impressions are usually correct, and why depression and other states of feeling are passed from mind to mind. Some delicately organized people find it inadvisable to go into society except at rare intervals; for they get entangled in these amospheres, and do not know how to throw them off. Others seem to have the happy art of leaving a part of themselves behind, of making every one else happy, yet never yielding their own personality to any contaminating influence.

But thought communications are not limited by time or space. One sometimes feels that a friend is about to call or write just before the actual visit is made or the letter received. People in different parts of the world working along parallel lines of thought sometimes make the same invention or discovery at the same time. The phenomena of thought transference are too well authenticated to need proof here, although I have the exact data of many experiences in my own life, and thought communication has long been a matter of common occurrence. The evidence in favor of a constant stream of mental influences passing from mind to mind is in fact overwhelming, and the mere data are not as important as the principle implied in their occurrence.

Some still dismiss such experiences as mere coincidences, or deem them of little value when the communication takes place between friends; but those who, like the writer, have taken note of the exact words, of time and place in which the message came, and have immediately received a letter from the distant friend containing precisely the same data, know beyond all doubt that the experience was no mere happening, and the very fact that such communications are common between those who are in sympathy is a proof of their occurrence. We recognize our friends' communications because we know their mental atmosphere. Other messages may come and produce no conscious impression on us, because we are ignorant of their source. They are mere impersonal thoughts, that slip into the consciousness almost as our own; and oftentimes we learn that these supposed original thoughts are common to the intellectual life of our time, and are "in the air." Whereas telepathic communications with a friend, like the sound of a familiar voice, have some meaning for us, and put us in touch with the friend's personality. It is not necessary, then, that certain words be transmitted and recorded in order to prove telepathy; for the mere directing of one's thought toward another is sufficient to make one's self known. In writing a letter, one naturally thinks of the person to whom it is to be sent; and this alone is sufficient to open up thought communication, and perhaps reveal the contents of the letter. The communication is its own evidence, and suggests a principle far more important than any experiential attempts to repeat it under exact conditions.

It is probable that we are living related lives, that we are not only members of one another through the all-encompassing Spirit, but that we are bound each to each by ties of thought. Mental man, then, is not an isolated creature any more than is physical man, but is part of a psychical organism, in which every thought plays its part and has its effect just as truly as the events in the physical world or in the social organism; or, better, that for conscious man there is but one organism, of which we contemplate now its physical, now its social, its mental, its ethical and spiritual phases, according to the line of thought or the self which chances to be uppermost. If this be so, and if the events of this purely mental phase of life be law-governed, correlated, and causally connected with its other phases, there can be no real chasm between mind and matter or between thought and soul or spirit. There must be some means of communicating between mind and mind, between thought and matter; and, while it is not possible to supply all the steps in the transition at this early stage of the inquiry, certain facts have already been ascertained which are of the greatest importance in the present discussion.

Many students of thought transference and of other facts of our mental life have found it necessary to postulate the existence of a subtle substance, which, like the luminiferous ether, conveys thought vibrations from mind to mind, precisely as the sun's energy is brought to our earth. It is far more probable that the communication takes place in this way than through the journeying of the soul from place to place; for, although some people have the ability to discover and describe things at a distance, there is little reason to believe that the soul ever leaves the body until the change called death occurs. Nor is it probable that the soul or spirit projects itself at any great distance. The thought wave probably passes through this finest form of ether, just as waves of sound are transmitted through the air, setting up vibrations in the recipient corresponding to those in the sender. Sound, light, heat, color, and the motion caused by wind on the surface of water are transmitted in this way; and one would naturally look for the same law in the realm of thought. In nature, then, it is the energy, the wave-motion, that is transferred, and not the object which gives rise to it. Every sound makes an impression on the atmosphere capable of setting up a corresponding vibration in the ears of all who are within a certain distance. In a similar manner each thought is probably registered on this subtle ether; and those who are open to it through sympathy or some common interest become aware of it or unconsciously receive the benefit of it. Minds of a like order are thus enabled to think together. The new thoughts of one stimulate those who are ready to respond, while thoughts that do not concern us pass off like sound in a desert, where there is no one to hear. Sympathy, receptivity, is the prime requisite in conscious thought communication. Yet, if there be an intermental substance, all minds must be open to it in some degree, and the most potent influences may be received unconsciously.

This ethereal substance in which our minds seem to be bathed is probably molecular in structure; yet it is obviously finer than electricity or the luminiferous ether, and is capable of penetrating the most minute spaces, just as the coarser gases interpenetrate the molecules of liquids and solids. It is evidently the finest grade of matter, and is immediately responsive to the slightest possible thought activity. On the one hand, it is probably like thought, or thought sent forth and condensed, just as the breath is condensed on a frosty morning, and on the other, like matter in its more ethereal forms. It may therefore be called thought matter or spiritual matter, since it apparently supplies the connection between spirit and matter, and partakes of both. In addition to the general intermediary between mind and mind there must then be a personal mentality, which gives shape to individual thought. This has already been in part described as mental atmosphere, and evidently proceeds from the personality, just as heat is seen rising from the ground on a warm day. It may be conceived as a wonderfully sensitive impression plate, jelly-like in texture, responding to the slightest possible change of thought, and performing an office similar to that of the earth's atmosphere, the minute particles of which catch the solar rays, and radiate them to the earth's surface in the form of heat and light. From it the transition is probably made directly to thought on the one hand and to bodily changes on the other, for it evidently penetrates the finest spaces in every portion of the physical body. Its existence therefore explains why thought can mould the body in causing and curing disease, and gives a reason for the supremacy of mind. In recent literature it is described as an uprush from the subliminal or subjective self; and it is probably in this surrounding atmosphere or uprush that faces, forms, and other shapes are seen, as well as a large class of phenomena known as hallucinations.

Whatever be the nature of this ethereal substance, it is evident, then, that it gives shape to thought. Dr. Quimby,* who, so far as I am aware, was the first to discover and describe this

*See Preface.

aspect of it, called it spiritual matter, since it possesses qualities characteristic of both matter and spirit. Into it, according to his description, are sown all sorts of ideas and erroneous opinions, fear, and beliefs about disease, which condense and germinate like seeds in the ground, producing changes in the body corresponding to the states of spiritual matter. He therefore distinguished between the mind which can be changed by thought and the mind which cannot change, which he called Wisdom. His own researches led him to make this distinction, and with him the existence of spiritual matter was no hypothesis, but a fact of experience. It was an object of perception with him. He could describe its changes, and was himself conscious of changing it when he explained some error to a person in trouble or sickness. His discovery therefore supplied the connecting link in the mental cause and cure of disease, which has been the means of relieving so much suffering during the past half-century.

It is evident, then, that this spiritual matter is also in close connection, if not partly synonymous, with the unconscious or, more properly, the subconscious mind, the physiological aspect of which is known as unconscious cerebration. The conscious thought evidently descends to the plane of the subconscious when it is dismissed by the will or the attention. It may then take form as spiritual matter, and be reflected in the body, or it may simply be turned over in the mind until the idea becomes a permanent factor in our mental life. It is a well-known fact that during this subconscious process new light is thrown on difficult questions, and the perplexing problem which we dismiss from consciousness at night is often solved for us in the morning. Whence came the new solution? Have we not arrived once more at the general conclusion of this book; namely, that "we lie open on one side to the deeps of spiritual nature, to the attributes of God"?* This openness is greater during sleep; and it is probably then that the mind gets many of its new ideas from the very source of wisdom, the mind that cannot change, the All-knowledge.

One mind is thus revealed within another, like organism within organism in nature. The problem becomes more complicated as we proceed; and in this great question — namely, the origin of our ideas — is involved the very mystery of life itself. But, not to complicate our present discussion, it is sufficient to say that this intermediary shades off into all the aspects of our life in mind. As it approaches the finest forms of matter in the physical body, it gives

* Emerson, "The Over-Soul."

rise to physical sensation, causing density, contraction, or expansion, according to the nature of the thought. As it vibrates or extends to other minds, it becomes thought transference, or, more accurately, the medium of thought transmission. Descending to the realm of the partly conscious, it becomes the subconscious mind, and is connected with the subjective or deepest self. Rising to the plane of definite thought, it blends with the conscious mind, by which it can be moulded like clay in the hands of the potter. At death it is probably separated forever from physical sensation, leaving the ability to communicate through its more spiritual aspect an indestructible quality of the soul.

Now that we have made the transition from matter to mind as well as our imperfect knowledge would permit, it becomes evident that the thought which changes matter is of far more importance than the actual process. There must then be some fundamental law which governs alike in our transitory and permanent mental states, and gives unity to the aspects of the inner life which we have passed in hasty review. As this law is of great practical importance, it is necessary to approach a definition of it by degrees.

If we observe a little child at play, we notice

that it turns from this sport to that, from one plaything to another, as rapidly as its attention is attracted. The first indication of definite growth in the baby's mind is this fixing of its baby eyes and its blossoming consciousness on some attractive object. The observant mother early learns to govern the child largely through its interested and skilfully directed attention. A little later she discovers that it is far better both for the present and the permanent good of the child never to call it naughty, and thereby to call more attention to its unruliness, but to interest it in some new play, or carefully and persistently to point out the better way, until it shall have become all-absorbing. Later still, when the child develops ways of its own, its persistence or wilfulness is still attention fixed on some cherished plan. The student so absorbed in his book that he is oblivious of the conversation going on about him illustrates the same power of a fixed direction of mind. The performance of skilled labor consists largely in the cultivation and concentration of the attention, together with the necessary manual accompaniment. The art of remembering well depends largely on the attention one gives to a speaker or book. That speaker or book is interesting which wins and holds our attention. That thought or event influences us which makes an impression, and becomes part of our mental life through the attention. We learn a language, grasp some profound philosophy, or experience the beneficial effect of elevating thought, rid ourselves of morbid, unhealthy, or dispiriting states of mind with their bodily expressions, in proportion as we dwell on some ideal or keep before us some fixed purpose, until by persistent effort the goal be won.

What is hypnotism but an induced direction of mind suggested by the hypnotist? When the subject is under control, and hypnotized, for example, to see a picture on the wall where there is none, the whole mind of the subject is absorbed in seeing the supposed picture, and there is no time nor power left to detect the deception. Many self-hypnotized people are equally at the mercy of some idea which is the pure invention of their fears. Insanity best of all illustrates the nature of a direction of mind pure and simple, with the wonderful physical strength which sometimes accompanies the domination of a single idea. All strongly opinionated people, those whom we call cranks, the narrow-minded, the creed-bound, the strongly superstitious, illustrate the same principle, and from one point of view are insane,— insane so far as they allow a fixed state of mind to control their lives and draw the stream of intelligence into a single channel: whereas the wisely rounded-out character, the true philosopher, is one who, while understanding that conduct is moulded by thought, never allows himself to dwell too long on one object, but seeks all-round development.

The point for emphasis, then, is this: that in every experience possible to a human being the direction of mind is the controlling factor. In health, in disease, in business, in play, in religion, education, art, science, in all that has been suggested in the foregoing, the principle is the same. The directing of the mind, the fixing of the attention or will, lies at the basis of all conduct. The motive, the intent, the impulse or emotion, gives shape to the entire life; for conscious man is always devoted to something. Let the reader analyze any act whatever, and he will prove this beyond all question.

The whole process, the law that as is our direction of mind so is our conduct, seems wonderfully simple and effective when we stop to consider it. Yet we are barely conscious of the great power we exercise in every moment of life. We are not aware that, in the fact that the mind can fully attend to but one object at a time, lies the explanation of a vast amount of trouble, and that by the same process in which we make our trouble we can get out of it.

Yet we know from experience that our painful sensations increase when we dwell on them, and that we recover most rapidly when we are ill if we live above and out of our trouble. On the other hand, we know that a wise direction of thought persisted in, or the pursuit of an ideal without becoming insanely attached to it and impatient to realize it, marks a successful career. Without the generally hopeful attitudes of mind embodied by our best churches, and expressed in our beliefs about the world, we should hardly know how to live in a universe where there is so much that is wicked and discouraging, and so much that is beyond our ken.

We are ever choosing and rejecting certain ideas and lines of conduct to the exclusion of certain others, and into our choice is thrown all that constitutes us men and women. The present attitude of the reader is just such a direction of mind; and this book, like the world at large, means just as much or as little as the reader is large and wise in experience. In the same way this book, or any other, reveals the life and limitations of its author. It cannot transcend them, it cannot conceal them; for in some way, through the written or spoken word or through thought atmosphere, personality ever makes itself known. The law of direction of mind is evidently no less exact than any which science has formulated. The world is what we make it, because only so much of it is revealed as we can grasp. In whatever direction we turn our mental search-light, those objects on which it falls are thrown into sudden prominence for the time. The world is dark and full of gloom only so long as we dwell upon its darkest aspects, and do not look beyond them. There are endless sources of trouble about us. On the other hand, there are innumerable reasons to be glad if we will look at them. We can enter into trouble, complaint, worry, make ourselves and our friends miserable, so that we never enjoy the weather or anything else. Or we can be kind, charitable, forgiving, contented, ever on the alert to turn from unpleasant thoughts, and thereby live in a larger and happier world; for the choice is ours. If we fear, we open ourselves to all sorts of fancies, which correspond to our thought, and cause them to take shape. If we communicate our fears to friends, their thought helps ours. If we get angry, jealous, act impetuously, we suffer just in proportion to our thought. If we pause to reflect, to wait a moment in silence, until we are sure of our duty, we experience the benefit of quiet meditation.

We invite what we expect. We attract what we are like. Let one understand this, and one need never fear. The law is perfect, and the protection sure. Our safety lies in **wisdom**; and, were we wise enough, we should probably have no fears at all. It is the explanation of our actual situation in this well-ordered world, dwelling near the heart of an omnipotent Father, that sets us free, and makes us masters of our own conduct. It should not therefore be a new source of terror to learn that we are beset by all sorts of subtle influences and hypnotic forces, or to be told that our own thought directions are largely instrumental in causing misery, dis-ease, and trouble of all sorts. These wrong influences cannot touch us. Our own mental atmosphere, our whole being, is a protection against them, if we have reached a higher plane. There must be a point of contact in order for one mind to affect another, some channel left open, some sympathy, just as there must be a certain affinity in order for two persons to form a mutual friendship. Our safety, our strength, lies in knowing our weakness, in discovering that the law of direction of mind is fundamental in every moment of human life. If after that we go on in the same old way, complaining, fearing, thinking along narrow lines, and submissively accepting the teaching of others, it will not be because we do not understand the law.

Out of the mass of impressions and opinions which for the most people constitute mental life, we can weed out those that bring harm, and develop those that are helpful. The economy of cultivating right thoughts is thus at once apparent. Matter is obviously just as much of a weight and a prison as we make it by our habitual thought. Looking one way, we enter into matter, or density. Looking in the other, we attract that which is spiritual, or quickening. Ideas have power over us in proportion as we dwell on them exclusively. It is a matter, then, of real economy, of necessity, to view ourselves and our habitual ideas from as many directions as possible, just as one goes away from home in order to break out of the ruts into which one inevitably falls by living constantly in one atmosphere.

Man leads a life of mind, then, because he is a conscious being, because the stream of consciousness is turned now into this channel, now into that, and can only take cognizance of a relatively large aspect of the world by the broadest, least prejudiced, and most open-minded turning from one phase of it to another. He has a distinct individuality, for which he is personally responsible, which it is his duty to preserve and to develop. It is through this, if he think for himself, that the keenest light is cast upon things; for it is the fundamental direction of consciousness, and ultimately blends with the

Self who knows all directions. Next in order comes daily experience, shaped by education, inherited beliefs and tendencies and whatever leads it into a given channel. After these fixed directions of mind come the mere fleeting influences, — mental pictures, fears, atmospheres, perplexities, and troubles, affecting the thought superficially, yet possessing a tendency to strike deeper into the being, and become fixed habits through subconscious mental activity. The law is everywhere the same; namely, that the conscious direction of mind, supported by the whole personality, is all-controlling for the time, since the mind can fully attend to but one object at once. Its application to daily life is at once apparent.

There is one consideration, however, which it is well to bear constantly in mind. The fundamental or ultimate direction of mind and the states of consciousness caused by the outer world are not of our own making: they are founded on the one Reality. We cannot wholly build the world from within. Science is trying to dispel all illusions, so that we may see it nearer as it really is. Our world is not a mere fleeting show. We cannot change it by an act of will or a simple caprice. It only yields within certain limits. Our world experience has a fixed and natural order. It is a system, both in its subjective and its objective aspects, a growth. Man is a progressive being. He is not yet completed, and the law of his growth is evolution. He may hinder that growth in a thousand different ways; and much depends on his attitude toward it, as we shall see in the next chapter. But he only changes the world as it appears to him, not as it exists in reality. Co-operation with it, with evolution, is his one greatest lesson. To learn how to adjust himself to the organism of which he forms a part is his great task, and the law of aspiration by which all evolution is guided is the direction of mind which is for him the one essential. His follies and fears will die of inanition. His harmful states of mind will cease to trouble him if he refuse them the attention which is their life. The source of the mental organism, in which he is a factor, is just as truly the immanent Life as the outer order of nature. It has a certain tendency, which he can follow if he will; and, if he follow it consciously and reflectively, his thought will constantly lead him back to the great Originator, in whom the worlds of nature and of our mental life become one.

V.

THE MEANING OF SUFFERING.

It was evident from the very outset of our inquiry into the origin and nature of things that we were considering a system, an organized whole. Events in that system move steadily forward with a certain rhythm. Everything is related to something else, cause leads to cause, and every fact suggests some relationship to an infinite whole. Indeed, it is difficult to see how a universe could exist unless its substances and forces were somehow unified in an ultimate, orderly whole, which should include them all; for a chaotic, an evil, and, therefore, a self-destructive universe is clearly an impossibility. A universe must be good,— that is, it must fulfil a purpose, intrinsically and extrinsically, in the light of the whole and in the light of the parts,— in order to exist. It must have a meaning. It must spring from a self-existent Reality, which knows that meaning, inspires that purpose, and is at least as orderly as the universe itself. That our own world-system is just such an orderly progressive whole is proved by the existence of an exact science describing it.

But what chance has man in such a progressive system? Everything seems to be determined. Long before he can take a hand in his career, fate has apparently chosen for him. Inheritance compels him to suffer for the sins of his parents. He is born into a world of misery, from which he vainly tries to escape. Life is a conflict at its best; and, even though he were free from the pangs of sorrow and suffering, there is a stern necessity which apparently carries him resistlessly forward to a destiny not of his own choosing.

One fact, however, of fundamental importance qualifies all that we know about the world of necessity. That world resistlessly makes itself known in a certain manner. But man is primarily a conscious being. He seems to be the product of environment, and his thought, his feeling, a mere ephemeral outgrowth of matter. Yet deeper than feeling, deeper than all that holds him in bondage to matter, is his individuality; and through this speaks a Power which renders all things possible. No two men are alike. No two interpretations of a world which is everywhere governed by the same laws are wholly identical. A personal element enters into every phase of human experience. Life, with all its pains and pleasures, is largely what we make it by our thought. Thought is a subtle moulding power, and is capable of directing or hindering the forces of nature. Behind the stream of consciousness is the human will, choosing and giving shape to it. The direction of mind is the tendency which gives shape to physical, intellectual, moral, and spiritual conduct. The idea is the foremost factor in every aspect of experience. These two facts — namely, that the infinite Power is trying to make something of us through our individuality, and that everything, happiness, misery, health, and disease, depends on our attitude toward that Power — explain the very mysteries of suffering and evil, at least so far as our limited knowledge can make them clear.

The first and most helpful thought to bear in mind, then, alike in the interpretation of a given case of suffering or evil and in those moments of pain when the soul reaches out for help, is that the Power is with us here and now, immanent in the very soul that needs help and in the very trouble from which we wish to be free. If one keep this realization ever in mind, remembering what that Power is and how it is made known, if one never forget the outcome, the meaning of it all, instead of dwelling on the sensations and the actual process by which one is becoming free, one's thought need never be oppressed by a sense of the stern necessity which compels one to suffer; nor will it become entangled in matter, as though that were the all in all.

Once more, then, the opinion we put into a thing determines its effect upon us. The direction of mind is fundamental. We become like that which we feed upon. If we go regularly to the theatre, if we read sensational and realistic novels, if we are intent on making money, if we live for pleasure or self alone, we draw the thought into a channel corresponding to the ideas on which the mind habitually dwells. If we associate with those who are morally and spiritually our superiors, we are made better by giving them our attention. If we investigate a certain line of phenomena alone, we become specialists, if not extremely narrow, in our way of thinking. If we reason, the world becomes rational to us; and our fears and vagaries die for want of an intelligible basis. Best of all, if we dwell upon the ideal Self, which is making the most of us it can, the whole life is made purer and more unselfish. But most vital of all is the thought of the last chapter; namely, that, if we look toward matter, toward physical sensation and disease, we call forth the energies in that direction, and build up through the subconscious mind and the spiritual matter a condition which corresponds to it, whereas, if we maintain a happy, hopeful state of mind, there is a corresponding expansion and lightness of the whole being.

The nature of suffering is therefore already in part explained; for, if our beliefs and directions of mind have such a powerful influence in the mere interpretation of matter, they must be equally powerful in determining our states of suffering. Recent literature has gone so far as to affirm that all disease is mental, a mere error of the mind. Yet it is evident from the foregoing discussion that the direction of mind is not all. It is the controlling factor, but is at times itself controlled. People do not consciously think themselves into disease or simply believe they have a certain malady. The subconscious mind, wherein we turn over and make our own the ideas and impressions that come to us, is a far more potent factor in our experience than the mere conscious thought. The influence of our opinions and habitual beliefs, our fears and traditional theories of disease, is so subtle, so closely connected with every aspect of life, that we are almost wholly unconscious of its power over us. We do not see how our states of mind can become translated into bodily conditions; and consequently we do not include these subtle effects in our interpretations of disease, until we learn that the direction of mind carries the whole energy of the being with it, because it takes form in spiritual matter. Human experience is most surely what we make it by our thought, but in that one word "thought" is involved the whole individuality and being of man. Our inquiry has taught us little if it have not shown conclusively that experience is a synthesis of objective and subjective elements; that even in the simple experience of physical sensation there is present not only the substantial basis for which the materialist contends, but also the thought, the conscious ego, which makes our life primarily mental. If the reader will bear this dual aspect of experience in mind, he cannot misunderstand this chapter.

It is clear, then, that suffering is a state of the whole individual. Every one who has given much attention to the subject of disease from this broader point of view must be convinced of this. In fact, from this point of view it makes little difference what the physical malady be called; for on the disposition of the patient depends the nature and intensity of the disease. Back of all chronic invalidism there is usually a selfish nature or one that is hard to influence, whose traits of character are made known in every aspect of the disease. On the other hand, an unselfish person, devoted to a life of self-denial, or one who is absorbed in congenial work, is apt to be freest from disease. Those who have time and money to be ill, those who live in and for themselves, and have nothing to take their thought away from physical sensation, never lack for some symptom out of which they can develop ill-health; and the whole practice and theory of disease are ready to co-operate in this process.

The very fact that so much depends on the temperament and beliefs of each individual renders it difficult to describe the causes of disease. Some people are so very hard to influence in any way, and are so tenacious of a condition when they get into it, that a very simple malady may be worse than a much-dreaded disease in a case where the disposition is pliable. The structure is tight and unyielding in many cases. People are too exacting, too intense in thought and action, or too opinionated and self-assertive to be easily moved. In such cases the struggle is always severe when it comes, and nature has a hard task to overcome so much rigidity. Many suffer from mere want of the action that comes from physical exercise. Some live too much in the so-called spiritual phase of life, and are out of adjustment to the every-day life of the world. Others are starving for spiritual food, and are in need of mental quickening, if not of severe intellectual discipline. Narrow religious opinions have a cramping effect on the whole life, both mental and physical. The tendency to nervous hurry is responsible for a large proportion of the more modern ailments. People dwell in fixed and narrow directions of mind, until they become cranky or insane.

Worry and fear play an important part in all varieties of disease, and some people have scarcely a moment's freedom from some tormenting belief or mental picture. Ill-will, want of charity, jealousy, anger, or any emotion which tends to draw one into self, to shut in and contract, is immediate in its effect; for, if it be continued, it disturbs the whole being, it is reflected in the spiritual matter, and finally in the body, where it is treated as if it were a physical disease. Unrealized ambition, suppressed grief, continued unforgiveness, dwelling in griefs and troubles instead of living above them, disappointments, and a thousand unsuspected causes, which impede the free and outgoing expression of the individuality, have a corresponding effect on the outer being.

We may as well turn at once, then, to the fundamental principle involved in all suffering; for there are as many kinds and causes of disease as there are people. Disease is not an entity which can seize us any way, regardless of our own condition. Whenever there is a disturbed condition which invites it, there is some cause of this disturbance back of the mere physical state, just as thought influences affect us through some sympathetic channel or not at all. Let us, then, define disease as mal-adjustment to the forces that play upon us, and see if this definition will hold true in all cases of suffering. If so, we shall find the road to health to be wise adjustment to the real conditions of life. We shall eliminate disease not by fighting it, not by studying its causes or doctoring its physical effects, but by seeing the wisdom of the better way. When we learn that it is a matter of economy never to rehearse the symptoms of disease, never to get angry, never to cherish ill-will, revengeful or unforgiving thoughts, never to make enemies, but always to be charitable and friendly, kind, good-natured, and hopeful, we shall not need to be told how we caused our own dis-ease; nor shall we need to say, "I will not think these wrong thoughts any more," for they will die out of themselves.

It is universally admitted that there is a natural healing power resident in the body. This power is common to all, or nearly all, forms of organized life; and by observation of the higher animals we have learned how thoroughly and quickly it can cure under favorable conditions.

Many people have learned to relax and to keep quiet, like the animals, by giving nature a free opportunity to heal their maladies. No one has ever discovered limits to this power, and some are firmly convinced of its ability to heal nearly every possible disease. It can knit bones together. If one meet with an injury or merely get a splinter into one's finger, it immediately goes to work in accordance with certain laws. There is a gathering about the injured part, and an outward pressure tending to expel any obstacle foreign to the body. Every one knows that the healing process is impeded or quickened according to the way we deal with it, and it becomes evident on a still closer study of the question that our opinions and fears have a strong effect upon this natural process. The whole process is simple and fairly well understood, so far as a mere injury is concerned. We rely upon it, and know how to adjust ourselves to it. But what happens when the equilibrium of the body has been interfered with in another way, and the vital functions impeded? Do we wait as patiently for nature to heal us as when we meet with an accident? No, nine times out of ten we mistake its cause, call it a disease which we think we have taken, misinterpret our sensations, and resist the very power which vainly tries to heal us. This resistance, intensified by dwelling upon sensation and careful observation of symptoms, adds to the intensity of the suffering, until the trouble becomes pronounced, if not organic or chronic. Yet all suffering is the same from the inner point of view, and should be treated in the same general way.

From this point of view the natural restorative power, the evolutionary force, or the spirit, in whatever form the immanent Life appeal to us, is ever trying to make itself known. On the physical plane it is ever ready to free the body from any obstacle or inharmony, and restore the natural equilibrium. It is continually purifying, cleansing, throwing off, all that is foreign. It is trying to free us from any inheritance which may cause trouble or suffering. It begins with us where it left off with our parents. Wherever we are weak, unfinished, undeveloped, that weak point, that undeveloped state, or that animal residuum, if one still be partly animal, and not man, is the seat of pressure from within of this same power, trying to make us better and purer. It ever penetrates nearer and nearer the centre of one's being, and the reason why a disturbance like the grippe is different each time it comes is evidently because the individual has changed. If one be exposed to the cold, to an atmosphere of contagious disease, of depression, or whatever the influence, the power is still there to protect and to heal. In all natural functions the power is with us, fully competent to secure their free and painless activity. It works through instinct and impulse for our welfare. On a higher plane it is operative in character, urging us to be unselfish, to understand the law of growth, and to obey it. On the spiritual plane it is ever ready to guide and to inspire us, but apparently, not so aggressive here, since so much depends on our own receptivity and desire to learn. On all these planes the power is pressing upon us from within, trying to expand from a centre, just as the rosebud expands or as the seed develops when its resident life is quickened. It is the power of God. It is beneficent, good, evolutionary, calling for trustful co-operation and restfulness on our part. We need not go anywhere or think ourselves anywhere to find it; for it is with us in every moment of experience, but usually unknown, rejected, and opposed.

If, then, it be asked why passion is so persistent, why evil has such power, why disease is so positive and real, there can be but one answer. The reality lies in the Power that is active with us, the suffering, the evil, the dis-ease in our mal-adjustment to it, in our ignorance of its nature and its purpose with us. There is something in us to be overcome, some obstacle, some inharmony. The restorative power is trying to free us from it; and, as it comes in contact with it, friction results. There is an agitation of the particles, made known to us as pain. This sensation we resist, not understanding it; and it becomes painful in proportion to our resistance to it. It grows more intense with every effort to endure it, to get rid of it, to doctor it; and so many sympathetic sensations are developed in different parts of the body, each with a different name, that it would hardly come within the province of this book to describe them. Everything depends on what opinion we put into the sensation at the outset; for the thought gives shape to the whole process, and either helps or hinders it.

To illustrate. The case was reported not long ago of a lady who was suffering with severe neuralgia. In her despair she was walking the floor, and her physician said the pain would not be relieved for forty-eight hours. Word came to her from one who had learned that much suffering is due to resistance to the remedial power to "let it come." The effect was immediate. The lady had been nerving herself to endure the pain, thereby increasing the intensity which first caused it; and the message revealed the whole process to her. She relaxed mentally, and surrendered the hold by which she had tried to endure the pain, became quiet, and fell asleep. This case is typical of a thousand others.

Again, those whose task it is to do considerable mental work learn after a time when they have worked long enough; for, if they work beyond a certain point, they become aware of pressure in some part of the head, from which a reaction is likely to follow. This is especially noticeable in learning a new language, taking up a study requiring close concentration, or any new occupation, art, science, or any form of physical exercise to which one is unaccustomed. One is soon conscious of fatigue, because the task is a new one, and habits have not yet been formed. The general tendency is to give up to the feeling of fatigue. Many become discouraged at this point, and give up study or exercise, saying that it makes them tired, and they cannot bear it.

What is this sense of fatigue? It is evidently due to the calling of power into a new direction. The new thought clarifies. It comes into contact with dense matter, with an uncultivated portion of the being, physical as well as mental; and, meeting with resistance, friction of some sort is the natural result. But this friction does not mean that one cannot exercise or study. It means the formation of a new habit and direction of mind, and the best work is done after one has passed this hard place. It calls upon one to wait a little while, and let the agitation cease, let the new power settle down and become one's own. It is nature telling one to be less intense for the moment, and to extend the limit of one's activity little by little.

It is a mistake, then, to give up to a feeling of fatigue and of pain. By giving up to it, one's thought is put upon it, with the result that it is increased, until the consciousness is absorbed in physical sensation. Rightly understood, pain is the conflict of two elements, a higher and purer element coming in contact with a lower, and trying to restore equilibrium. It is remedial. It is beneficent, the most beneficent of all nature's arrangements, the best evidence of the unceasing devotion and presence with us in every minutest detail of life of a resident restorative power. Through it we are made aware that we have a life not wholly our own that cares for us, and is capable, perfectly competent, to take us through any possible trouble, since it is there only for our own good, since it is itself thoroughly good.

But it is obviously the power that one should think of, and not of the sensation. In this way, if one be determined to see the good, to think of the outcome, one will live out of and above the sensation; for all these thoughts help. **The consciousness is either turned in one direction or the other. It either helps or it hinders.** One either moves with, thinks with the current of life, or tries to stem it. In one direction the thought is turned into matter, in the other toward spirit. In one direction toward self, with a tendency to withdraw, shut in, contract; in the other, toward the higher Self that is with us, telling us to be wiser, toward all that is happy, hopeful, and expanding.

These two mental attitudes may be illustrated by the sensation one experiences on a very cold day. When one comes in sudden contact with the cold, the first impulse is to shiver, to draw in and contract, whereas all who have tried it know that by simply letting it come, by opening out instead of shutting in, one does not feel as cold, and no harm results. In the former case, as in all instances of suppressed grief, fear, or any emotion which causes one to withdraw into self, that which has been shut in must be opened out. This the natural restorative power tries at once to do. A pull or a painful sensation in some part of the body is the result; and, mistaking the sensation, the person, full of fear, contracts more intensely, causing the sensation to increase, until nature can only restore equilibrium by a violent reaction, which receives the name of some well-known disease.

But why do we resist ? why do we withdraw into ourselves and into consciousness of physical sensation? Obviously, because we are ignorant of the Power that is moving upon us. We have been educated to believe that disease is a physical entity. We put the wrong thought or some borrowed opinion into our feelings. The fears and sympathetic words of friends help the process. The possible symptoms we are likely to suffer are graphically described, the memory of past experiences of suffering is called up, until finally the whole diseased condition is pictured out before us, and the thought is every moment becoming more firmly fixed in the wrong direction. Our whole environment tends to keep us in ill-health; and disease is literally made by man out of a simple condition, from which nature would have freed us had she been given opportunity.

In order, then, to understand how we resist and cause our own suffering, we must recall the central thought of the preceding chapter. Life is primarily mental. It is the conscious ego that knows and feels the suffering. The sensation, the pain, the suffering, is in consciousness. It is mental, and every conscious state is interpreted according to the wisdom of the thinking ego behind it. Here is the starting-point of all subsequent experience in the outer world.

As we start, as we believe, as we think, so will be our experience, our suffering, or our good health. The reader need only pause to consider all that this means, to see the full bearing of a state of mind, in order to understand the whole process; for the entire personality, education, temperament, and the physical activities are carried with the direction of mind, and, if the direction be into matter, into the belief and fear of disease, nature has just so much more resistance to overcome.

The leading thought of this chapter will therefore be lost unless the reader understand disease from its mental side, unless it be clear that the whole process is mental; for, if this discussion have simply called up pictures of suffering and the memory of the reader's own struggles, without showing what lay beneath them, it has wholly failed in its purpose, and aptly illustrated the power of a wrong direction of mind. We are in search of a way out of suffering; and, if it is now clear that the entire mental attitude enters into our diseases, causing resistance and pain, it must also be clear that the same energy sent out in the right direction will be of the greatest help in securing health.

Here is a vital truth. The discovery that by maintaining a quiet, trustful, reposeful state of mind, inspired by genuine understanding of the process that is actually going on, the whole being is kept open, permitting the natural activities to operate unimpeded and without suffering. It is of such vital importance that the remaining chapters of this volume will be devoted to a consideration of this most helpful attitude, and how to maintain it. Here is the turning-point away from matter, mental pictures of suffering and theories of disease into spirit and the stronger, purer, higher life, where one never speaks of one's self as diseased, but where the same Power which once made itself known through suffering, because one opposed it, now causes good health, because one moves with it. Here is the way of escape from the narrowing thought of life in the present, in time, into a hopeful realization of what one's experience means as a part of eternity; and, when one contemplates the end, the outcome, one is no longer entangled in consciousness of the means, the process.

The first point to note is that one cannot judge by physical sensation, but should look beyond it. In sensitive natures the sensation of pain is very much exaggerated, and is no guide at all. Sometimes the sensation is so keen and the pressure reduced to such a fine point that one's consciousness is like a caged bird fluttering about in a vain endeavor to escape. Shut in there with such intense activity, the wildest fears are aroused when there is no real cause for alarm. The trouble is simply very much restricted. The Power is pressing through a very narrow channel; and relief will come in due time if one be quiet, patient, not trying to endure the pain, but letting the Power complete its task.

The second point is to remember that the resident Power, or Life, is always with us, and to think of that Life instead of dwelling upon our troubles. What a change would come over the moral world if this realization were to become a permanent factor in daily life! for there is obviously no exception to the omnipresence, the love, of God. If one accept the doctrine of God's immanence, there is no logical stopping-place in favor of the elect. If God dwells with one, he dwells with all, consciously or unconsciously. If he has some purpose with one, he has some meaning in the lives of us all. No man, then, is inherently wicked. There are no heathen. No one is lost or ever could sink so low that the same Spirit that had a meaning in his sin could not carry him through it to a conscious realization of what that meaning is. Once more the vital question is, What is the divine meaning of it all? For, if a person or an act has a meaning, that person or deed is not and cannot be wholly evil, and to say that any act of wickedness happens despite the divine power is to deprive that power of the very infinity and wisdom by virtue of which both God and the universe exist. When the emotions are touched, the struggle is apt to be very intense, and more likely to be misunderstood. The immanent Life, moving upon man where he is weak and undeveloped, through instinct, passion, and impulse, produces restlessness, which in turn causes him to rush now into this thing and now into that, and perhaps commit a crime even before he is aware of what he is doing. The very tendencies and instincts which would guide him in his development, if he understood them, are misdirected. An impulse blesses or curses, according to the opinion of it, the attitude towards it, and the way in which it is followed, blindly or intelligently. Man never conquers himself by self-suppression any more than by indulgence, but by adjustment to the forces of his own being.

The meaning of much of our moral suffering and evil is, then, to teach the right use of our powers; and moral misery and degradation will probably continue until the lesson be learned. All cases of sickness, misery, evil, wrong, demand better self-comprehension. If there be one general meaning which applies to them all, it is, in one word, progress,— the effort of the Spirit to give us freedom. If we understood this, we should have a larger sympathy and charity for the whole human race, and be spared much suffering over the sins and crimes of others, and should look for the meaning, the Spirit, behind all wrong acts and all degraded lives.

The one great question, then, in all problems of suffering and evil, whether in personal experience, in history, in the animal world, or in present human society, is this: What is God doing with us? What is the ideal toward which the immanent Life is moving through us? All secondary questions reduce themselves to this; for everything goes to show that the universe is a system, an organism, an adjustment of means to ends for the benefit and development of the whole, inspired by one grand purpose, and proceeding from a Spirit that put all wisdom into the great world-plan. We did not make the world-order. We cannot change it; and, if our life in it be full of misery, it is for us to discover how we make that misery, how we rebel, how we resist, and what the order means for us and through our lives.

If a nation be torn by internal troubles, by wars and wrangling of conflicting parties, it is evident that it has not yet learned the great lesson of human brotherhood, and that its troubles must continue in one form or another until it discover what the evolutionary energy means, what it is trying to make known through these very conflicts. Our own nation, standing as it does for freedom, progress, and industry, has already made a great advance toward this larger fellowship as compared with its more warlike neighbors and competitors. It will undoubtedly be the first nation also to settle the conflict between rich and poor; for here, too, it has brought the issue forward more rapidly than other nations. It is learning one of the great lessons of evolution; and the poor must suffer until the two classes learn their respective and brotherly relations to each other, their need of each other, and their common goal.

Contest and controversy will continue in the same way between science and religion, between the great religions and the sects into which many religions are divided, until men learn that all truth is one and universal, and does not depend on any book or any person, but is the inherent property of all, trying to make itself known through these very controversies, and revealed in every fact of life. Theory and practice will also be at variance until it be clear that they are one, that what a man does he believes, regardless of his boasted theory. Impulse or instinct will be man's guide until he learns what is behind it, until he stops to reflect and to act intelligently with, not against, the forces of his own being; for thoughtlessness is the besetting sin of man. A large proportion of the crimes committed by him would be prevented if he stopped to consider the consequences, not only the suffering which would be caused to others, but his own severe punishment, caused solely by his own acts, because action and reaction are invariably equal.

Suffering, then, is intended to make man think. Behind all experience moves one great aspiring Power, developing and perfecting the world. It moves straight toward its goal unceasingly and without permanent hindrance. Wherein man is adjusted to it, he is already free from suffering. He moves with it, and knows how to be helped by it. But wherein he still acts ignorantly, he suffers, and is obviously sure to be in conflict until he understands the law of growth. Man has been defined as a pleasure-loving animal. He is lazy, and will postpone thinking for himself or try to shift his responsibility until he learns that everything depends on the development of individuality and of individual thought. But a day comes when he begins to reflect and to see the meaning of it all.

Everywhere, in the outer world, in history, in politics, in religion, he finds two forces contending with each other. Turning to his own nature, he finds the same, a higher, a rational, a moral and spiritual self contending with a lower, an impulsive, an animal self. He sees that he must obey the one and neglect the other, or, better, lift the other to a higher plane. He sees that evil is a relative term, depending on our point of view, and that conduct which seems perfectly justifiable on one plane of existence is condemned on a higher plane, where different standards prevail. It becomes clear that virtue or goodness can only be attained through an experience full of contrasts and friction, an experience which calls out the best that is in us, — true sympathy, love, and character. The meaning of his own mysterious past becomes clear. He sees the rich compensation for all that he has suffered in the wisdom and character it has brought him. And, finally, in this far-reaching adjustment of means to ends he recognizes the love of God, and proves to his own satisfaction that love really dwells at the heart of the universe.

The discovery, then, that there is no escape from the operation of cause and effect, neither mental nor physical, is a turning-point in the progressive career of man; for the majority still persuade themselves that they will somehow be excused. Suffering is only necessary to bring us to a knowledge of the law, to bring us to a certain point; and it will persist until that point be reached. Our experience of to-day is conditioned by our past life. It is what we have passed through which alone makes it possible for us to stand where we do to-day. Consequently, what we do and think to-day will largely govern our experience of to-morrow and of all future days. Fate has not decided everything for us after all; for it was by our own consent, unconsciously, thoughtlessly, and consciously, that we suffered. Our fate is that through our individuality something is bound to come forth, for the resistless power of Almighty God is behind it. Our freedom lies in choosing whether to move with progress or against it; for man may evidently continue to sin, to oppose, and misuse the very power that would bless him, and to postpone the lesson which at sometime and somewhere he is fated to learn. If, then, in any case the result will sometime be the same, it is a matter of economy to learn the real course of events as soon as possible, since the law of action and reaction is eternal.

As hard, then, as it may seem to be compelled to suffer the results of our own unwise conduct, it is in this discovery that we learn the meaning of suffering and the way out of it. Once more, then, we must look beyond physical sensation to the conscious man behind it, choosing, willing, determining his conduct and his pain or pleasure by his direction of mind. It is impossible in one chapter to consider suffering in all its phases; but, if this central thought be clear, if the reader has stopped to consider the intimate relationship of God to man in every moment of life, these neglected problems will be equally clear, for that relationship must be universal. Not all suffering is evolutionary. Not every evil act has its discernible meaning. Most of our suffering is purely incidental, passing off without leaving us any the wiser; but all suffering, all evil, may become evolutionary. Every slightest experience will teach us something if we question it, and will yield its message of hope. This is the chief value of all experience and of the present discussion; for the final meaning of suffering is hope, the last word of this chapter is "hope," the message of the Spirit as it speaks to us in moments of despair, in times of trouble, throughout life, throughout history, in all evolution, is a grand inspiring Hope.

VI.

ADJUSTMENT TO LIFE.

In one of the most secluded of Alpine valleys, where the steam whistle has never broken the native stillness, nor the progress of science intruded on the confines of mediæval tradition, lies one of the most remarkable villages in the world. The traveller, as he enters this unique town, feels that he has suddenly stepped into another world; for the people inspire him with an unwonted reverence, and an atmosphere of Sabbath stillness rests over all the valley. One all-controlling idea pervades the town, and is alike absorbing to every man, woman, and child that lives there. The village is Oberammergau; and here once in ten years representatives of all civilization come to witness the world-renowned Passion Play. For hundreds of years this play has been given ten summers in a century by these simple peasants, and their entire lives are devoted to preparation for it. To take the part of the Christ is the summit of their ambition. They feel it a solemn duty to give the play, and from childhood their lives are shaped by this ambition. In order to represent a certain character, they practise the most careful self-denial. They try to mould their lives in accordance with the qualities of that character, and they dwell on it and rehearse it year in and year out. And this is why they are so remarkable. They are shaped by an ideal. They have one object in view, and in their peasant simplicity and catholic faith they are willing to exclude every other. When they appear in the play, they make no affectation. They simply represent in actual life what they have so long dwelt upon as an ideal. And this ideal has left its stamp on everything associated with the town and its people.

It is a rare privilege for the student of the human mind to be among these people for a time, and to witness the play; for there in actual practice and in striking simplicity is the ideal of all character-building, of all co-operation with evolution, of all adjustment to life,— namely, to have an object in view which we never lose sight of, and which we gradually realize, day by day and year by year. Life for the most of us is vastly more complicated than for the peasant of Oberammergau; but the principle of character-building is just the same, and just as simple and effective.

What this principle is we have been considering from the very start; that is, to learn the real conditions of our progressive life, to gain some knowledge of the deepest law of our being, and then to conform our conduct to those conditions and that highest law. We find ourselves part of a great Reality, made known to us through internal and external sense, everything which reveals it being real. This simple act of consciousness, even though we know the Reality immediately, is immensely complicated; and our interpretation alike of its nature and of its meaning depends on temperament, education, mental and physical surroundings, and a hundred other conditions. Opinion, belief, fear, prejudice, hypnotic influences, and various subtle forces enter into and color our thought. We misinterpret sensation. We become the prey of our own fancies, and yield to the stronger minds about us. We are ignorant of the forces that play upon us, and consequently are not adjusted to them. We suffer, and we witness a vast amount of suffering which we seem powerless to prevent. But one law characterizes our conduct both in health and in disease. The central thought in consciousness for the moment or through habit, the direction of mind, shapes our lives, so that we really lead a life of mind. We live in a world partly of our own making, partly the product of all past evolution, both mental and physical, but a world which happily reveals a progressive order to which we can adjust ourselves in co-operation with the Spirit behind and within it, a world which has a purpose, a meaning with us, and with our individuality, which experience is trying to make plain.

It is evident, then, that at every step in our inquiry we must discriminate between the higher Self which never changes, which has a meaning in our lives, which possesses us, needs us, is sufficient for us, and the lower self which is constantly changing, obeying now this whim and now that. In proportion as we make this discrimination and obey the higher Self are we free from conflict and suffering, and adjusted to life. If we abandon our fears, cease to complain, to rebel, and learn the real economy of our situation in life, then this higher Self has free access to us. It meets no opposition. Its purpose is made known without suffering. We enjoy the only true freedom in co-operation with the omnipresent Helper, whom we once despised. Gradually, a simple system of conduct and of adjustment to life takes shape in our minds, until, like the peasant preparing to take part in the play, we know no other ideal. To suggest this ideal so far as one person can indicate it for another is the purpose of this chapter.

But let us first be perfectly sure that we understand how conduct is shaped by an idea.

When we leave our home, for instance, to go to the business portion of the town or city in which we live, it is usually because we have some definite object in view. Our conduct for the time is guided by a transient desire; and, in order to carry out this desire, we adjust ourselves to a certain arrangement of natural phenomena, and make use of certain mechanisms invented by man. We take a car or carriage. We are compelled to follow certain streets in order to reach our destination. We must avoid collision with other people, with electric cars and carriages. We must good-naturedly take the situation as we find it. And all these actions are governed, almost unconsciously to us, by a single desire; and we keep this end in view until we attain it.

Thus we might analyze the conduct of any day or any moment, and find that wish or desire controls everywhere. In learning a language, we keep the object in view of reading and speaking it with fluency, and calmly work for years until we attain it. We make an invention because we need or desire it. The need or desire opens us to the means of fulfilling our wish. The artist has an ideal in view which he is ever striving to realize on canvass or in marble. Literature takes such form as our desires give it, modified by the degree of cultivation we have attained. We change the character of our buildings, of our homes, of our institutions, our philosophy, our religion, our conceptions of the divine nature, just as rapidly as we ourselves change, and to the degree that our ideals and circumstances are modified by these inner changes. We endeavor to understand nature, life, history, our entire surroundings better. We then readjust ourselves in conformity to our better wisdom. And in every wise readjustment we are compelled to adopt nature's sure and measured method of evolution. We look for changes in and through the very conditions of politics and society, of moral and spiritual degenerateness, which we once sought to revolutionize from the outside.

All this seems simple and evident enough when one's attention is called to it. But do we follow this easiest and most natural of methods when we try to transform character and to secure better health by mental means? Are we not apt to say, This shall be so; to exert our wills, to forget the higher Self, to strain after ideals, to claim that which is not yet true and can only progressively become so, to expect to transform ourselves too quickly, to dwell in thought somewhere way off in the clouds or in the distant future, instead of wisely adjusting ourselves to the eternal now? Is the will really so powerful that it can abolish time? What is the will, and what is the nature of its power?

When I raise my arm and move my hand, the various motions which I am compelled to make seem to be controlled by my will. Yet I know very little about that apparently simple process. The hand and arm are moved by certain muscles, the muscles by a certain nervous discharge, which obeys definite laws utterly beyond the power of my will to control. I simply desire my hand to move in a particular way; and, lo! a wonderful mechanism, perfected by nature long ago, is set into activity. The complex motions by which I move my arm and hand are matters of habit rather than of will, and I use nature's mechanism almost unconsciously. The whole body responds to my thought in the same manner, and the great outside world goes on almost regardless of my will.

What, then, is my will? Has it no power? Simply this, says the new psychology, as expounded by Professor James,— attention. "Whatever determines attention determines action." The child ceases his play, and turns his whole activity in some new direction because his attention has been attracted. We thread our way among the obstructions of a busy thoroughfare because our thought is fixed on some distant object. The hypnotist shapes the conduct of his subject when he has gained control of the subject's attention.

Will is a direction of mind with a definite object in view. It is the mental or conscious side of physical conduct, and as such it wields great power. It is thought fixed in and calling force into a given channel. Will uses power. It gives definite shape to power. It opens one to power, so that "I will" is equivalent to "I am ready." A person with a strong will is one who persistently keeps a desired object in view. The human power lies in the desire, the divine or natural in that which fulfils it. Here is a very important distinction. By longing for an object we unconsciously put ourselves in an attitude to attain it. We gravitate toward it. We exclude everything else in our efforts to attain it. All else is merely overdoing the matter.

Again and again we forget that will is a directing power, and act as though it were a force which we must exert. But my will alone is powerless to move my arm. I will to move it, and at the same time co-operate with nature's mechanism and my own well-established habits. If I kept saying, "I will move it," "Now I will move it," it would remain motionless. By saying, "I will do this," "I will have things thus and so," we are apt to get into a nervous strain, to assert our own power, our own selfishness, as though the human will were all-powerful. Self-conceit and ignorance of the larger and diviner life accompany such self-assertion, and close the door to the higher power. The Spirit quietly withdraws at the approach of such assertion.

The little flower, bursting from the bud into the glad sunshine, lifts up and opens itself to the light and warmth. It is openness, readiness, receptivity that is demanded of us. The thought put into the mind at night which wakes one at a given hour in the morning has its effect if we trust, not if we are anxious lest we oversleep. New ideas and new power seldom come to us while we scrutinize our mental processes and try to catch and to control the inspiration as it comes. But ideas and wishes sown in the mind like seed seem to have a wonderful power of growth and possibility of fulfilling our desires. The wisely chosen ideal modifies our life by a scarcely discernible process when it is thus sown in confidence and expectation. We only know that in a thoughtful moment we saw our error, and concluded that it would be wiser to act thus and so, and then dismissed the thought quietly and trustfully.

The process is wonderfully simple when it is not overdone, as the little boy digs up his garden day after day to see if his seeds are growing.

Some have mastered it sufficiently so that the night's rest depends largely on their last thoughts before losing consciousness in slumber, or have learned to control the thoughts of an entire day by giving them wise direction in the morning. There is a wonderful possibility here for those who learn how to co-operate with their own deepest evolution, through wise and trustful adjustment to it. It is probable, too, that a large part of our troubles and many a painful malady would be cured by the same simple means if we could once learn the art of patient, restful adjustment, if we would let nature heal us without resistance or interference. But we nerve ourselves to endure, and thereby resist nature's remedial power. We are impatient to get well, forgetting that there is a natural law of recovery, and that nature tends to restore the lost equilibrium as rapidly, and only as rapidly, as it can be done well.

There is a difference, then, between ignoring a trouble, between neglecting to take proper care of ourselves, and that wise direction of thought which in no way hinders while it most surely helps to remedy our ills. There is strong reason for believing that there is a simple, natural way out of every trouble, that kind Nature, which is another name for an omniscient God, is ever ready to do her utmost for us. We can go through almost any experience if we feel that the power residing within is equal to the occasion. When we cease to look upon any experience as too hard, we have made a decided step in wise adjustment to life. Life itself becomes easier and happier when we make this grand discovery that within each human soul there is a sufficient resource for every need along the line of the individual career. We can conquer anything that lies between us and our destiny. It would be strange, indeed, if, granting that an infinitely intelligent Spirit sent us here for some purpose, this were not so. It would be strange, too, if any experience in the individual career were without its meaning in the divine economy. If, then, we can assume this, too; if, in place of the cruel fate which, as we thought, cheated us out of our just dues and defeated our hopes, there is a larger Fate that somehow needed for us just what we passed through, there is no room for regret, no cause for complaint, since in regretting and complaining we are finding fault with Omniscience itself. It is not for us to say that life is not worth living. Our life, such as it is, belongs to a grander Life, to which we must ever turn in order to see the meaning of our own. And experience becomes infinitely pleasanter the moment we realize the futility of all regret, complaint, and opposition.

It is equally necessary to note the difference between wise adjustment to circumstances which for the time being we cannot alter, and that utter contentment and ease in our surroundings which leads to inactivity and invalidism. Some people are too well adjusted to their environment. They need a sudden stirring, like an alarm of fire, to wake them up. They do not grow. They are selfish, and lack even the rudiments of true self-denial, as though the world existed for their own benefit. Or perhaps they are self-satisfied, and fail to see the need of further mental evolution. They are very well contented, polite and agreeable, so long as nothing comes to disturb them; and they take care that nothing shall disturb them, so far as their power extends. If they are sick, every one must become a servant. Every sensation is watched and carefully nursed. Everything must give way to their wishes. Everybody must help the matter on by expressions of sympathy and devotion. But place such people on their own resources, put them where something does come to disturb them, and they are utterly helpless. Progress brings conflict. We need to be stirred once in a while, and put where we must show what we are really worth. Then comes the real test. If we are adjusted, not to some transient set of circumstances which we personally try to maintain undisturbed, but to life as a whole so far as we understand it, we shall be able to meet any emergency, to meet it manfully, trustfully, and contentedly. There is no better test of one's philosophy than at these times, when we are called upon to act as if we believed it true. There is no better way to prepare for such emergencies than to meet the circumstances of daily life as though we were superior to them.

It is a matter of economy for ourselves, it is a source of happiness to ourselves and our friends, if we habitually look for the good wherever we go, and in this way show our superiority to all that is belittling and mean. We shall soon find no time left for complaint and discouragement if we undertake this happy task with a will. We shall discover new traits of character in our friends, new sources of enjoyment in trivial things, and new pleasures even in the weather, that potent cause of useless complaint and regret. New beauties will reveal themselves in nature and in human life. We shall gradually learn to see life through the artist's eyes, to look for its poetry, its harmony, its divine meaning.

The traveller in foreign lands is compelled to meet experience in just such a happy mood as this. He knows that each day is bound to bring its annoyances; and he determines to meet them philosophically, and, if possible, to see their comical side. In a foreign land one makes it an occupation to hunt up all that is curious and interesting. The spirits are quickened, enthusiasm is aroused; and one notices a hundred little effects, changes, and beauties in sky and landscape, on the street and in people, that are passed unnoticed at home. We make note of them in order to describe them to our friends. Imagination lends its charm even to the most disagreeable experiences, and all our journeyings stand out in the vistas of memory painted in golden hues.

Such experiences should give us the cue in looking for the good at home. It is well, too, in matters of disagreement with friends, to preserve the same large spirit and breadth of view, remembering that we have more points of agreement than of disagreement with them, that we all belong to the same infinite Love, and all mean the same great truth; but we cannot quite say it. It is rather better to be tolerant, to have a large charity for people, than to expect them to be like ourselves. One person of a kind is usually enough. God apparently needs us all. Those who have learned to think, especially those who realize the meaning of evolution, are usually aware of their faults; and **encouragement is what they** most need. People do nearly as well as they can under the circumstances and with their scant wisdom. If we know a better way, it will become evident to them if we practise it. If they offend us or get angry, we have all the more cause for charity and good feeling. We need not suffer in such a case unless we put ourselves on the same plane, and get angry, too. There is no quicker or more smarting rebuke than to receive an affront in silence or in perfect good feeling. There is no better evidence of a large and generous nature than immediately to forgive and to forget every injury, and thereby to be superior to the petty feelings of resentment, pride, and unforgiveness, which work mischief alike to the one who holds them and to the one who has done the injury. We are surely to blame if we suffer, since everything depends on our own attitude.

If we thus give our attention to building up character, broad, charitable, and true, the wrong thoughts will disappear through mere lack of attention. Psychology once more helps us here, and says that we can attend to but one object at a time. Science tells us, too, that in the evolution of the animal world organs which remain unused ultimately disappear, while the development and perfection of an organ accompanies its use. We need not then reason our erroneous thoughts away. Usually, it is sufficient to see that we are in error, to learn that all these fears, resentments, morbid thoughts, and complaints affect our health and happiness. The explanation is the cure.

Nor is it necessary to analyze sensation and try to discover the various moods that cause our trouble. No one who has passed through the torments of self-consciousness, to find only one's own insignificant self looming up through the introspective mist, like a repellent spectre from which one would fain be free, will ever advise another to brave these torments. The human self with the divine Self as a background is the only picture of the inner life which one can bear to look at long. This picture will paint itself. The other is of our own vain contriving. In those moments of calm reflection when one ceases to analyze self, and lays aside the cares of the busy world, the deeper consciousness will be quickened. One falls into a gentle reverie. Pleasant memories and mysterious experiences come before the thought. One sees wherein one has failed to practise one's truest wisdom, or sees the meaning of some experience that seemed hard and inexplicable at the time. Then, as one gradually turns in thought from personal experience to the larger experience of humanity in its relation to the great Over-Soul, all these varied events and personalities will be knit together in relations unsuspected before. One will have new glimpses of truth,— that deeper truth which comes unbidden, but which is ever ready to make itself known when one is intuitively awake and receptive.

A synthesis of these spontaneous reflections will give one more genuine knowledge of self than any purely introspective process. And likewise in any moment of trouble or sickness, when we need help, it is better to open out like the flower, receptively, quietly, expectantly, conscious of the nearness of the divine Helper, than to pursue our own thought, and try to solve the difficulty. We are too active as a rule, too sure of our own way, too much absorbed in our own plans and fears. The Spirit demands but little of us, quiet, lowly listening; but it does ask this much. Here is the real power and value of silence. All that we perceive in these happy moments spent in quiet reflection has a lasting effect upon us. It is then that we grow. It is then that ideals take shape, and become permanent directions of mind. It is then that we get newly adjusted to life; for, after all, this task is never completed. Something new and perplexing is ever coming to test us; and always there is this one resource, to find our inward centre, and there to stand firm and contented.

It is also in these more deeply reflective moments that we learn our own limitations and possibilities. We become aware of that deepest tendency which lies at the basis of temperament and personality, through which the great Spirit speaks. We learn a deeper and truer self-reliance, which ultimately means trust in God. We learn through experience when to obey this inner moving and when the impulse is merely our own personal desire. In a word, conduct reduces itself to one simple rule: Study to know when you are moving along the lines of your own deepest nature, your own keenest sense of what is wise and right, and when you are off the track. It is right and necessary to have certain standards by which conduct may be judged, to have a philosophy which teaches one to look on all sides of an issue and to reason carefully. It is well to look to friends, to public teachers and books, for help in all humility and willingness to learn. But standards vary. The conscience of a people changes from age to age. Even intuition must be verified. It must find support in reason, and undergo the test of experience. The surest and simplest method, for those who have become aware of such guidance, is to await the divine emphasis, to act when the whole being speaks, to move along those lines in which no faculty of one's being interposes an obstacle. All ultimate questions of right and duty should obviously be settled within the sacred limits of one's own personality, where the great God speaketh, if he speaks at all. "The soul's emphasis is always right," says Emerson.

To some this doctrine may seem the essence of individualism, urging one, as it does, to find a ready resource for all trouble in one's own nature. Yet, rightly interpreted, it is by no means selfishly exclusive, any more than that ideal of human society towards which, in the opinion of many thinkers, the present evolution of the social order has all the while been tending; that is, it seeks to give the individual mental freedom and free opportunity for development within the limits of what is required of him as a member of society. We have thus far considered the problem of adjustment in its simplest form. All that has been said in the foregoing chapters properly enters into the question,—the nature and relationship of the immanent God to his manifestations, and all that we know about those manifestations. The world is an organism. Society is an organism. Human minds as well as human customs and social institutions are evolving together. One by one, and individual by individual, we are knit together in one great mental, social, and universal fabric. Each need, each aspect of the organism, the adjustment of part to part and of means to ends, demands special consideration. We owe certain duties to ourselves in order to preserve our physical well-being, in the fulfilment of which we are aided by all that science has discovered concerning the human body, its evolution, its care, and the need of exercise. We owe other duties to our fellow-men in order to preserve the well-being of society; and in this we receive greater aid each year through the rapidly advancing theories of moral conduct, of universal religion and sociology. We need and long to know what is right in all cases, to know what is our duty. Ethics enters into every act and thought of human life. We owe it to ourselves, to our neighbor, to the universal brotherhood or the divine fatherhood, to be doing something in particular all the time, to choose this line of conduct and reject that. And this knowledge of duty should rest on a scientific interpretation of the universe, on a study of life in its total relations, including the discovery, so far as we can make it, of whither events are tending.

No one can think deeply about life without considering these larger issues. But, even in approaching the problem of adjustment in its simpler and more individual aspects, we discover many ways in which we can pay our large debt to society. One cannot develop very far beyond the less thoughtful masses without leading them on; and, since man is an imitative creature, there is no surer way of helping him than by setting him a nobler example. Our uncharitable, our fault-finding and fear-carrying words and thoughts are just as harmful to others as to ourselves. When we overcome these wrong habits of thought, our friends will not be slow in noticing the change. With the advent of a wiser habit of looking for the good, of getting encouragement out of everything, and of disposing of our troubles in a quiet way ourselves, instead of burdening others with them, the reaction on our associates will prove wonderfully helpful.

This doctrine, then, says in a word, Be unselfish; have an ideal outlook; see yourself as you would like to be, healthy, happy, well-adjusted to life, helpful, wisely sympathetic, and ever ready with an encouraging word, looking for the good, growing strong in wisdom and power, patiently awaiting occasions, yet always sufficiently occupied, so that you will have no time to be annoyed, fearful, restless, or morbid. It points out new ways in which we can be of service to our fellow-men. It makes us aware of our own responsibility, and shows us that life is an individual problem. It warns us never to look upon that problem as too difficult to solve, if we approach it moderately, hopefully, and full of cheer.

Is it not a duty we owe ourselves and other people to be supremely happy, forever young in spirit? We have all met those whose very being seems to thrill from some unseen source of happiness, who seem to know by instinct that all is good. What influence can resist such a power, and what trouble can long weigh down such a bounding spirit? It is like the glad song of the birds, which will not let us be melancholy, or the feeling of worship for the source of all good, which wells up in the presence of some beautiful landscape. It is health. It opens one to the renewing, the indwelling energy, by which we exist, whereas fear contracts, and causes one to shut out that energy. There is something profoundly unhealthy in our thought if any trouble whatever leads one to suppress this happy tendency. Its source is eternal, its spirit perennial. Its power in counteracting the selfish and morbid tendencies in life is boundless. It is not to be sought for its own sake alone. It is not the end of life. It is rather the spontaneous accompaniment of the highest usefulness, the deepest worship, the truest love, the greatest thankfulness, the profoundest repose and trust in

God. It is the truest sanity. It marks a well-balanced mind. Science and philosophy do not always satisfy the soul. Reason leaves room for doubt. Pessimism and despair are ready to follow, if we do not check them by some happy thought. The greatest assurance, the one that never fails, is this indefinable somewhat, this happy restfulness, which no doubt can shake, this feeling that we are right, this sublime faith, this unfathomable intuition, which leaves no barrier between the soul and its perennial source. A sense of trust and thankfulness wells up with this deep assurance, a feeling of joy in the blessing of existence, which defies the subtlest scrutiny, which unites the simplicity of childhood with the profoundest reaches of manhood's thought. It is well to take note of its conditions when it comes, to observe what a range of thought and sentiment is opened up by genuine happiness, and then, when the spirit of depression weighs heavily upon us, to recall these conditions, to let the morbid thought languish for mere want of attention, to stir one's self, to arouse a forced happiness if one cannot shake off the heavy spirit in any other way.

It is a matter of economy to be happy, to view life and all its conditions from the brightest angle. It enables one to seize life at its best. It expands the soul. It calls power to do our bidding. It renews. It awakens. It is a far truer form of sympathy than that mistaken sense of communion with grief and suffering which holds our friends in misery instead of helping them out of it. It is a far nobler religion than that creed which causes one to put on a long face, and look as serious as possible. Once more, there is something wrong in our philosophy if it sanctions melancholy and pessimistic thoughts. We have not yet looked deep enough into life. We have never got beyond being impressed by the sadder and gloomier side of life. We are still thinking and acting contrary to, not in harmony with, the happy world of nature by which we are surrounded. By maintaining this mournful attitude, we show our want of faith in the goodness of things as much as when we fear. A deep, unquenchable spirit of joy is at once the truest evidence that we believe in the beneficence of the Father, and that we have penetrated deep enough into life's mystery to see how best, most economically, most courageously and helpfully to take it.

Patience, too, is a word that suggests much that is needful in the adjustment to life. Hard, indeed, is it for some to abide nature's time, hard to eliminate the idea that creation was completed long ago. Consider for a moment the vast age of our fair earth, how many æons of cosmic time it revolved in space ere vegetation appeared, and then pass in imagination down through the long cycles of struggle and development which led the way to the production of the first man, a creature with whom we would not own kinship. History is still young. It is made to-day with unwonted rapidity, and one can hardly keep pace with the advancing times. Yet nature is just as moderate as ever, and our century is but the bursting bud of ages of measured preparation. Long ago the ancient Greeks spoke for beauty of form. Long ago Jesus spoke for the beauty of service. Not so long ago Luther spoke for freedom of conscience and reason. Slowly the great world is brought round to the perception of these great prophets, who stand like guide-posts, indicating the will of the Most High.

Progress is just as measured in human life. We cannot hasten matters. We may as well accept the conditions of progress as we find them, and not postpone our lesson. My experience of to-day is the outcome of my experience of yesterday, of my past life, and is conditioned by it. My intuition tells me of grander experiences to come. It furnishes ideals. But I cannot enjoy those experiences now, I cannot **realize** the ideals now, because I cannot **omit** one step in my progress. I am ready, in the full sense of the word, only for the step which logically follows the one I am just now taking. I must not overreach nor get into a nervous strain. I must not let my thoughts dwell on the future. I must not be anxious nor assert my own will, for I do so at the peril of my health and happiness. I ought rather to live in the eternal now, and to understand my experience in the light of cause and effect. I must build my new future by gradual modification of the shifting present. I must select and reject, choose and neglect.

For, despite the fact that this endless chain of causes and effects, whereof my fleeting experience is a part, is law-governed and fate-driven, I have a wonderful amount of freedom. I can not only choose between accepting life's conditions trustfully, contentedly, making the most that is good out of them, and rebelliously complaining at them all, I can not only make of the world what I put into it, and thus regulate my own happiness and misery, but I can cause infinite misery to other people. I can sin, I can degrade myself lower than the animals, I can be thoroughly wicked and mean,— all within certain limits,— I can make of myself what I will; but I can never escape the torments, the inevitable results of my own acts. Not all the creeds, not all the good men, not all the prayers and sacrifices in the world, can ever change natural law, or save me from the heaven or the hell which I am preparing for myself by my daily conduct. What I am thinking and doing day by day is resistlessly shaping my future,— a future in which there is no expiation except through my own better conduct. No one can save me. No one can live my life for me. It is mine for better or for worse. If I am wise, I shall begin to-day by the simplest and most natural of all processes to build my own truer and better world from within. As surely as the great world of human thought comes round to the position of one man, so surely does the whole fabric of personal thought and action respond to our will. We have only to wait, to be patient, to renew our ideals day by day, to remember that ideas have life, regenerative life, and a natural law of growth. Nature and our own subconscious mind will do the work for us.

Here, then, is evidently the secret of the whole matter. To look persistently toward the light, toward the good, toward what we would rather be, and as we would rather feel when we are suffering, with some happy prospect in view if we are morbid, with some deed of kindness in mind if we are idle and in need of something which shall absorb and fix the attention. Such will-power as this is irresistible. It is the God and one that make a majority.

Adjustment to life, then, is an individual problem, and varies with temperament, surroundings, and habits of thought. Its principles are universal. First, to realize in our own way the truth of Chapter II., that there is but one Reality, or God; that we live in God; that God lives in us; that he is completing us, moving upon us through the forces, the events, the world in which he resides, through our weaker nature, through our faults, through the conflicts which we have so long misinterpreted, through pain, through happiness, and all that constitutes experience; that we have no power wholly our own, but that we use and are used by divine power; that we are equal to any task, any emergency, any struggle, for that great Reality is all there is. It is all power. God is here. Help is near. We need not go anywhere for it. It is omnipresent. It abounds. It comes to us in proportion to our receptivity to it, our faith in it, our happiness, our hope, our patience. Then to choose wisely what we wish to be in co-operation with the immanent Life, since "whatever determines attention determines action"; to see one's self not in the introspective, but in the divine light; to be practical in the choice of ideals; to be ever happy, ever young, ever hopeful, and never discouraged. Conduct is thus the conscious adjustment of our acts to the purpose of the deeper Self so far as we know that purpose.

But can we practise all this? If we could, our doctrine would be of little value. We must have ideals,— ideals which we can begin to realize to-day; and our discussion has been of some use, if it has shown the necessity of moderation, of quiet, trustful imitation of the methods whereby the great world of nature has come into being.

Every one who has dwelt for a season in that joyous world of the larger hope, where one is lifted above self, above space and time, so that one seems related to the revolving orbs of space and to the limitless forces of the universe, knows that there is a sudden, almost painful descent to the realities of every-day life. Life is a constant readjustment. It requires a daily renewal of one's faith, and then a return to the tasks, the struggles, which at times well-nigh weigh us down. It means repeated failure. It means a thorough test of all that is in us. It often means trouble and discouragement whenever one gets new light and regenerative ideas, since a period of darkness similar to the decay of the seed in the ground follows every incoming of greater power. But it is priceless knowledge to know that we are equal to the occasion. It is a long step toward self-understanding when we learn to see in facts that once caused discouragement profound reasons for hope and cheer. It is a decided step toward self-mastery when we learn to meet these ups and downs, these regenerative periods, in a broadly philosophical spirit, at once superior to our circumstances and to the thoughts and fears which once held us in their power. It is fortunate, indeed, if we no longer deem life's task too hard, if our faith be sufficiently strong to sustain us through the severest tests, thereby proving our fitness to be made better, our willingness to persist, though all be dark, with an iron determination to succeed.

VII.

POISE.

THE one essential, alike in the interpretation of life and in wise adjustment to its inevitable conditions, is the knowledge that there is one, and only one, Reality, whose being therefore transcends and includes our own and all that can ever form an object of our thought. All else is contained in this, all else follows from this, if we pursue our inquiry far enough to learn what that Reality is and how it is made known. The supreme problem is to know how best, most economically, most healthfully and happily, to take the eternal order, not simply as we find it in the outer world, but as it is made known within as a part of the life, of the very consciousness and substance, of that one Reality. For, if this is literally true, if the world-system is the self-realization of an infinite God, it behooves us to know it, to make this knowledge the guiding principle of life, since the universe cannot then be a world sent out from Deity, apart from him, the product of mere caprice, to be some time destroyed, when the caprice shall change. It must endure as long as eternity shall last. It could no more be destroyed than the self-existent Reality, whose consciousness it is. The world-plan could not be changed without departing from the highest wisdom and purest love which God must possess in order to be the one Reality.

There is the strongest reason, then, for taking life as it really is in this largest sense, since it must be part of the best possible world-plan in order to be a fact at all and be self-preserving. Everything that occurs in your life and mine must have some meaning in this world-plan, for nothing could come forth at random from an infinite wisdom. There is no other reality, and we have no independent life. To let this one purpose have free expression through us, so far as it relates to our individual career, — this is life in its deepest and happiest sense, this is health and poise.

But, before considering this final element in the problem of adjustment, let us ask, What is to be the ultimate outcome of life's aspiration? What is the real meaning and purpose behind all these mysterious experiences and trials? Is it not the development of a soul, and is it not for lack of spiritual self-possession that we are whiffed about by opinions and fears? What is a soul? One may as well try to define the larger Self, from whom, as we are persuaded, the soul's noblest aspirations come. Yet we know perfectly well what we mean until we are asked to define it; and we have some conception of that eternal realm of thought, superior at once to space and to time, where the poets and philosophers dwell who speak words of comfort to the soul. Our own deepest reflection transports us there, and we seem larger as a result of our meditation. There are experiences that call us out of and above ourselves, noticeably those that make one acquainted with grief in its larger sense; and the soul seems to expand with the new experience. We know when, on the one hand, a man's soul speaks through his words, and when, on the other, he says one thing with his lips and thinks another, thereby trying to conceal his soul. The whole being speaks through a perfectly genuine act, through truly ethical conduct. We mean something genuine, something honest, appealing, and true, bespeaking that indefinable thing called personality. It is a part of what we call character and temperament. It is that which endears one to those whose life gives us a glimpse of God, and makes one feel assured that life, if it produces such a thing as this, is well worth all its hardships. It is the test of all that is dearest and truest in human experience. It is that which transcends, yet gives unity to the physical, the intellectual and moral man. Through it comes that wisdom which leads men to act better than they know, which bids one be calm when there is seemingly reason to fear and grieve, which assures one that all will be well even when reason opens the way to the profoundest doubts. It is the meeting-point of the eternal, never-changing Spirit with the ever-varying experiences of human life; and many feel confident that we are far enough on the eternal side, so that life will be continuous from this experience on, so that we can affirm personal immortality.

Our deepest life, then, is a continuous incoming of renewing, sustaining power welling up from the heart of the universe into the spirit of man, a continuous, divine communication engaged in the rearing of a soul. The deepest self is not physical, nor even intellectual. It is spiritual. We are spirits now, in germ it may be; but, in so far as we are conscious of our life in God, that consciousness will probably never be broken. Man is not a body with a soul, but a soul or spirit, which in every well-poised person is master of the body and of the powers of thought.

Now, if the soul stands uppermost in importance, it is our first duty to keep the soul on top. Many people work so hard at their vocations that their souls have no room to expand. They are lawyers, doctors, financiers, with whom business stands first, not men in this spiritual sense of the word. Anything which subordinates the soul, and prevents man from taking all that belongs to him as a free spirit in a beneficent world, any mistaken sense of humility or self-suppression, has a harmful effect on the whole life, and is evidently as far from a normal attitude as strong self-conceit. If one have continued impulses to do good, and suppress them, a reaction is sure to follow. It is better to express the impulse, even in a slight way, if one cannot realize one's deepest and fullest desire. Theological creeds often suppress the soul. One feels a desire to be larger, freer, and to think for one's self. Want of charity, continued fault-finding, the attempt to do a task that is beneath one, narrows the soul. Love, of the truer sort, broad thinking, open-heartedness, happiness, expands it, and has a marked effect on the health. Sacrifice of individuality to the control of a stronger mind suppresses the soul. Education often crushes out originality.

Now, we were evidently designed to be free, to have strong, manly individuality. It is well, therefore, to consider wherein we are held down by people and circumstances, and to discover how we are cramping our souls. The soul should be master, and the powers of thought should be free. Do we not yield part of our manhood or womanhood the moment we give way to worry, to continued grief or discouragement? On the other hand, is not the realization of what we are as living, growing spirits, who use the body as an instrument, and control it by thought, who dwell with God and need never fear any permanent harm,— is not this the way to free ourselves most rapidly from all that would hold us down? We have all experienced those calmer moments when we quietly faced our fears, our doubts, and our wavering opinions, and as calmly dismissed them, henceforth powerless because we saw their utter absurdity. Half the battle is won when we see our error, and realize the possibilities of the soul. We are momentarily masters of the situation. We are more truly and profoundly ourselves, we discover our inner centre, and become poised, grounded on eternal reason and calm in eternal peace. This is at once the highest use of the will and the truest spiritual self-possession; for it is in these moments of calm decision, when we realize our relationship to eternal power, that the mind changes, and brings all things round to correspond to our deep desire. The ideal of daily conduct is to maintain this inward repose, to keep it steadily and persistently in view, to regain it when we lose it, to seek it when we need help, to have a calm centre within which is never disturbed, come what may,— a never-yielding citadel of the higher Self.

It is evident, then, that the whole of human life, and all that we have considered in the foregoing chapters, may be restated with deeper meaning in terms of soul, or spiritual, experience. The soul must learn what it is and why it is here. It must gain this knowledge by actual experience, in order to learn the value of right conduct, in order to learn that there is a Wisdom, a Love, that is equal to all occasions. It must descend into density, or matter, and become acquainted with darkness and sin, in order to discover the meaning of life and become conscious of itself as an individualization of God. It struggles upward and forward to completion. It is ever trying to come forth and express itself; and, when man comes to consciousness of what it means to develop a soul, and of the divine trend in his personal life, he no longer resists this deep moving. He comes to judgment in his own soul, and sees how he might have acted more wisely. With this deeper consciousness comes readjustment to life and more soul freedom. His soul finds better expression through the body, not in some future existence or in another body, but here and now; for even its experiences in the flesh are soul experiences, and demand, not punishment in the flesh at some distant time, but better and truer conduct in the eternal now.

If anything is purposeful in the universe, then it is the life, the aspiration and character, the soul of man, as it passes from stage to stage in its progressive experience, unfolding and giving to the light the divinity involved in its very being. It is the knowledge of this permanent factor in so much that is passing and trivial which gives one poise and strength to pass through any experience without fear that it may prove too hard.

People disturb us. They narrate their troubles and describe their sensations with painful minuteness of detail. Crowds, city rush and noise, deprive us of our peace. Be as watchful as we may, we find ourselves going off on a tangent, on a tirade of fear, or on a round of gloomy thoughts. We are misunderstood, illused, and wronged. Our faith is tested to the utmost, and we are pushed to the wall. There is obviously just one wise course to pursue in all such cases. Not to be disturbed, not to enter into the painful narration, not to rush with the crowd nor to countenance gloomy thoughts, not to feel uncharitable, revengeful, or unforgiving, since one will only add more trouble, but to regain one's poise by such thoughts and realizations of who we are as progressive beings, and what the Power is that is with us, as the occasion may suggest. Find your centre, learn to know your home in God and what he is doing with you, and you can safely let the great world go on, and let nature's organism right all wrongs and heal all hurts.

I need hardly remind the reader that it is not so-called will power that invites this repose, but the higher and truer will explained in the foregoing chapter; for self-assertion plainly defeats one's object. People who are strong in themselves alone obviously have no poise in this deeper sense, as a soul experience. Those who reach out after the ideal as though it were somewhere afar off and not immanent in the real, who look forward to the future with a nervous strain instead of living in the present, where help is alone to be found, lose what little poise they have, and fly aloft on a burst of enthusiasm. The consciousness is concentrated wherever we send our thought; and, if we reach out or pray to God as a distant being, the thought is sent away from its proper sphere. It were better not to have ideals at all than to strain after them, and assert that they shall become facts at once; for nature's method of measured transformation through evolution is the only wise and health-giving course to pursue.

To know that everything we need is within, here and now, this is poise. Realization, not assertion, is the method of this book,—a realization which teaches through actual communion with it that there is an omnipresent Wisdom to which we can turn at any moment and in any place, of which our being partakes, and which is so near to us that we have no wisdom, no power, no life wholly our own.

We are so accustomed to think of the divine nature as wholly unlike and separated from our own character that it is long ere we can make this realization a fact of daily consciousness. We have taken credit to ourselves for qualities which inhere in the very Essence itself. We have limited our worship of God to one day in the week, to one place of prayer, and sought his revelation in one book. Dogmas have crystallized about us, and we have hardly dared to think for ourselves. Yet a little reflection shows that we are, that we must be, partakers of an omnipresent Love; that not the Bible alone nor any other sacred book, but every book through which the soul of its author speaks untrammelled, every divinest impulse, all that spurs man on to progress, all that is most sacred, is a revelation of God, for he is not an exclusive, but an inclusive God. This being so, we obviously do not know ourselves, do not possess ourselves, and have no

permanent centre of repose, until we discover this inward kingdom of heaven.

When we discover it, life seems just so much the larger and better worth the living. We learn that there is something within that will teach man better than any mere thought of his own, that he has a wellspring of guidance and inspiration in his own soul. It gives quietness and comfort to know this fact. Nearly every one has had such guidance at times, sudden warnings of approaching danger and impressions not to do this or that; and help has often come to us during sleep. But this realization of the nearness of All-knowledge gives a reason for such experiences, and encourages one to believe that they can be cultivated and relied on. Then, too, it gives one confidence and strength of a truer sort, not in self, self-consciousness, and the products of one's own intellectual development, but in that larger Self which is crowded out by all sentiments of pride and self-satisfaction. One loses fear, one ceases to worry about one's friends and to suffer for wrongs that one is powerless to prevent, when this realization becomes a fixed habit of thought; for, if God, and not man, is behind events, we can safely trust the universe to him, and not only the universe, but our friends, our suffering and ignorant fellow-beings, and our own souls. The sense of officiousness is displaced by a feeling of patient trustfulness, and we spare ourselves a deal of unnecessary suffering; and I need hardly add that one not only gains greater repose, but that the health is immensely benefited, since the disease-making directions of mind no longer have a chance at us.

Education of the truer sort brings poise; for it develops individuality, health, and strength of intellect, which in turn means health and strength of body. Physical exercise, music, or any line of work which rounds out the character and acts as a balance wheel, is essential for the same reason, since it draws the activities out of narrow and therefore unhealthy directions of mind. Those who are very intense in disposition often find it necessary to exercise vigorously, in order to counteract this extreme mental activity, until by degrees they become less and less intense, and learn to work moderately and easily. There is an easiest, simplest way of doing everything, with the least degree of strain and nervous anxiety. We do not learn it while we hold ourselves with the grip of will-power, when we try to work our brains, and force the activities into a given channel. "Self-possession forgets all about the body when it is using it." It interposes no obstacle to the physical and **mental forces.** It discovers the easiest method of concentration through inward repose, and finds in this quiet restfulness the greatest protection from nervous reaction and fear.

Poise, then, is a word of degrees. Many have it on the physical plane, and are apparently seldom disturbed in their physical life. Systematic physical exercise brings control of the muscles of the body, and with this control a certain degree of poise. In learning to play a musical instrument, one gains it through long training; and we say of a great musician that he has repose, that he plays or sings without effort. But one may have bodily repose, yet have no repose of character, and may be the victim of a veritable whirlwind of nervous excitement within. Those who are aware of their own mental development and soul growth are usually conscious of touching a deeper and deeper centre, and with each experience comes added poise and readjustment to life. Every trying experience demands a strengthening of one's faith or a deepening of one's self-possession; for the natural tendency is to fear, worry, and doubt. We are not sure of ourselves until we have met and undergone the test of a severe experience. Any experience, then, that strengthens this inward repose is rather a blessing than a hardship. Is it too much to say that we can become equal to any experience whatever, and meet it unmoved within, in quiet trust and perfect faith? Surely, the possibility is worthy of our consideration.

If we have proved to our satisfaction that two and two make four, and that the result will always be the same, we are undisturbed by those who affirm that the result should be five. So far as we have rationalized experience and discovered certain laws, our conviction is no less certain, because nature, like mathematics, is a system on which we can rely. If the reader is convinced that God is immanent, or that evolution, so far as science has described it, is a true statement of life's process of becoming, this knowledge furnishes a basis on which to reason. It gives poise and inspires trust. To be sure, the conditions may change, and other forces enter in to counteract and modify the results in a given case. To the forgetfulness of this fact is due the tenacity with which some people cling to their beliefs, simply because they are unaware of these modifying circumstances and causes. Doctors seem justified in affirming that disease is a physical thing, that organic and chronic diseases cannot be cured by mental means, because as a class they are unaware of the deeper aspects both of the cause and the cure of disease. But the exceptions only go to strengthen our faith, since every effect is like its cause, unless a new element be introduced. Then it is invariably different. The laws hold true universally; and, if the reader has grasped the few great but highly important laws of human life, he can now rise superior to moods and experiences, troubles and illness, which once would have caused fear, doubt, and a great amount of unnecessary suffering. Simply to know that every event has an adequate cause, that action and reaction are equal, that experience depends on our attitude towards it, and that with a change of mind, a new directing of the will, the forces of our being are brought round to correspond with it,—without any further effort on our part,—this simple knowledge is enough to give us poise, and make us masters of our fate.

One's method of adjustment to life or one's optimism need not necessarily be the philosophy of this book. There are as many approaches to it as there are temperaments, and this is just the point of this chapter. Have a method. Have a soul of your own. Be your true self. Think, realize, reflect, until you have a measure of unborrowed conviction, which establishes a centre of repose, and is a source of happiness and contentment,— a centre which yields to no outer tumult, but is ever receptive to the divine Self; which never harbors fear or doubt, no matter what the wavering self may say; which never wavers, never forgets that the individual belongs to the Universal, never relaxes its hold of the deepest, the truest, the most spiritual in life, come what may, be it sorrow, illness, or any calamity which life may bring; a centre which you will probably discover at last rests on the love of God for its strength, making it part of eternity and of all power and substance, though it be but a point in the infinite whole. And, when you lose this poise, regain it, as though you would say, "Sit still, my soul: thou at least must not lose thy composure nor thy awareness of the eternal presence of God."

Those who are nervously inclined will find it necessary to stop themselves many times a day when they discover that they are under too great pressure. They will find themselves hurrying unnecessarily or inwardly excited. Oftentimes all that is needed in order to prevent serious mental and physical trouble is to take off this pressure, and find this quiet inward centre. It is wonderfully refreshing and removes fatigue to relieve the pressure and open the spirit to the healing power. Simply to turn away from self, and all that destroys repose, to the Self which knows nothing but peace, is sufficient to give one help and strength at any time and in any place. The wise direction of mind opens the door to help. If we trust, if we expect it, the help will come, whereas the effort to make it come will put an obstacle in its pathway.

To know how to rest, this is the great need of our hurrying age. We are too intense, too active. We have not yet learned the power and supremacy of the Spirit, nor the value of quiet, systematic thinking. We struggle after ideas. We read this book and that, and go about from place to place in search of the latest and most popular lecturer, instead of pausing to make our own the few great but profoundly simple laws and truths of the Spirit. We are unaware of the power and value of a few moments of silence. Yet it is in our periods of receptivity that we grow. Not while we actively pursue our ideas do we get the greatest light. Oftentimes, if the way be dark, and we can get no help, it is better to cease all striving, and let the thoughts come as they may, let the Power have us; for there is a divine tendency in events, a tendency in our lives which we can fall back on, which will guide us better than we know, if we listen, laying aside all intensity of thought, and letting the activities settle down to a quieter basis. Here is the vital thought of this book, its most urgent appeal to suffering humanity and the soul in need. Part of its teaching can only be verified by experience, and must seem merely theoretical to many readers. But here is a thought that is for every one, a simple, practical thought, that leads to and includes all the rest. Let us pause for a time, think slowly and quietly, and not leave it until we have made it our own.

Silence invites the greatest power in the world, the one Power, the one Life. Let us be still in the truest and deepest sense of the word, and feel that Power. It is the All in all. It knows no space. It knows no time. Its slightest activity is universal and eternal. It surrounds us here and now, in this present life, this beautiful world of nature, of law and order, this inner world of thought and the soul. It is the supreme wisdom and perfect love. It knows no opposition. There is naught to disturb its harmonious, measured, and peaceful activity. It is beauty and peace itself. Its love and peace are present here with us. Let us then be still. Peace, peace, there is nothing to fear. In this one restful happy moment we have won the peace of eternity, and it is ours forever.

Who that has communed with the Power of silence in this way can do justice to the unspeakable joy of that one moment of rest and peace? It is not a thought alone or a suggestion that brings it. It is something more than so-called thought. It is inner stillness. It is the receptivity of the soul. It opens one to the thing itself, the eternal Peace. Many will find it difficult at first to banish other thoughts; and it is better not to force the stillness to come, but to let the agitation cease by degrees, letting the thoughts come until they quiet down for mere want of conscious attention. When at last the thought no longer wanders here and there, but is poised in the present moment, and the feeling of peace becomes uppermost, it is better to cease definite thought altogether, and simply enjoy the silence. One will then have a sense of incoming power and of newness of life which no other experience can bring. This may not be the result at first, because it is only after repeated trials that one learns how to become still. One may even be made more nervous by the simple thought of stillness. It is often easier to realize this peace for another than for one's self, but the result will in time be the same. The consciousness will be drawn away from self and physical sensation; and this, after all, is the one essential, to rise above self into the nobler world of altruism and the Spirit.

Some have found it helpful to set aside fifteen minutes each day for quiet receptivity of this deeper sort. Then, when times of trouble and suffering come, one will not lose one's self-possession, but will know how and where to find help.

The instance is related of a student in the university of Leipzig who was in such an intense state of nervous strain that the students and professors were much alarmed at his condition. By some good advice he took up the habit of sitting quietly by himself for about fifteen minutes each day, in absolute silence, maintaining as nearly as possible a state of perfect composure and muscular rest, banishing all thought and all activity. In a short time he made a very noticeable improvement, and finally recovered his health. The mere effort of maintaining an easy, relaxed state of mind and body had relieved him of the inward pressure. He had unconsciously realized the power of silence, and it had healed him.

If one fails utterly at first to gain this silent repose, and becomes still more restless, one should not feel discouraged. That is just the moment to rejoice and to know that one has succeeded. The experience is the same in all efforts of reform. The first result is to stir up and encounter opposition.

Suppose for a moment that the reader is impatient, and, seeing the error of his ways, decides to exercise self-control. Very likely he will lose his patience on the very first occasion, and act or speak impulsively. Discouragement naturally follows; and the reader forgets one of the great laws of growth,—the law, namely, that a period of darkness, of regeneration, of sharp contact with all that can rouse itself into opposition, follows the reception of new light, of greater power. Conservatism and habit are ever ready to rise up, and say that there shall be no reform. All healthy changes are evolutionary, not revolutionary. We forget that an idea, like a seed, has life, and, if sown in the mind, will grow. We forget the outcome. We often falsely accuse ourselves of sin, when the relapse is really due to a firm determination to be better. If we keep the end in view, if we have an ideal outlook, we can safely let the disturbance be what it may. Quiet persistence is the word. Each effort to renew our ideal adds to its evolutionary power. "Keep your eye fixed on the eternal, and your intellect will grow," says Emerson.

One's first real success in attaining this inner repose sometimes comes alone with nature when, standing in silence under the pines and thinking in harmony with their whispering or awed by some grand mountain scene, one freely and fully yields to the spirit, the calm, the rhythm of one's surroundings. Afterwards one can return in thought to the mountain summit, where the eternal silence of the upper air was so deeply impressive. Or one can imagine one's self by the sea, where the ceaseless ebb and flow of the surf on a sandy shore once quieted the troubled spirit, or afloat at sea on a beautiful June day, listening to the regular play of the waves along the steamer's side. Any thought which suggests silence will produce the result, until one gets in the habit of thinking in harmony with the rhythm of nature, just as one can learn to rise and fall with the motion of a steamer as it responds to the steady waving of the ocean.

Everything in nature seems to have its ebb and flow, its alternation of day and night, of activity and rest, the one blending into the other throughout the seasons and the centuries. The strains of a grand symphony carry one in thought to this region of rhythmic alternation. One is glad enough at times to lay aside present problems and everything that is modern, and read the great authors who wrote for all time, or read some history or scientific work which transports one to the past, and gives one a sense of time, of the long ages and the periods through which the earth has passed and man has worked his way.

There seems to be a corresponding rhythm in human life, with its ups and downs, its joys and sorrows, its successes and its failures. Yet the interval is often too long for our short-sighted discernment. In the night of trouble and despair we forget that the day will surely dawn again. We occasionally emerge into remembrance of what it all means, and we think that now at last all will go well. Then comes the descent. We are plunged once more into the depths, where the facts of life are seen at the close, pessimistic range; and once more our memory fails to hold over. But in due time these contrasted experiences fall into a system, if we reflect on their meaning. We are awed by the eternal fitness of things. A stronger hand and a profounder will than our own is revealed in the fabric of our soul, which no purely human effort could have knit together. We are almost ready to affirm that whatever is is right.

It is true we make many apparent mistakes. Within certain limits we seem to have an infinite choice. We are conscious of wrong-doing. We deliberately sin sometimes, and we have much to regret. Yet a time comes when many of these experiences yield up their meaning. We justify mistakes in the light of their outcome. Each hour of conflict had its place in teaching part of life's great lesson. A world of truth flashes upon us through the memory of some wrong act; and we question the wisdom of the slightest regret, since we have acted so much better than we knew. This soul-experience, this personal evidence that we have been guided, is for many the strongest assurance that our world-order is the best possible order. They are conscious of being led to certain lines of conduct at the right moment. They see their humble place in the world, and await the next step in quiet expectancy. One may as well tell them they have no eyes as to deny this inward guidance, for it leads them from task to task with a certain system. If it does not tell them what to do, it at least opposes no obstacle, like the famous dæmon of Socrates. It either speaks definitely or it opens the way to the soul in repose, not the soul that thinks it knows how to act, and gives the deeper Self no room to speak. One cannot hasten it. One cannot always discern the proper course until the proper moment. It often comes unexpectedly, causing humility and surprise that so much should be given us. But the right thought comes in the fitness of time to those who quietly await it.

Thus one is drawn at last out of the narrow prison of one's own self-consciousness and physical sensation into this larger thought of the whole. It gives rest and trust to feel one's self part of a fabric so wonderfully and systematically woven, where the world-plan is not alone concerned with the selfish needs of one man, nor the wrongs which one would like to see swept away because we do not see their meaning, but with the total needs of all as related to the total universe.

One loses all sense of time and space under the power of this grand thought of the transcendent wholeness which shades off into eternity. This transient thought of ours, this divine moment of time, is a part of that eternity. It links the limitless future with the irrevocable past. It is just as important, just as truly a part of eternity, as any moment could ever be. We learn that we are in eternity now, not that it is something to come. We try to comprehend what it means, in eternity now, in infinite time, in boundless space, or, better, above all time and space, where one Power, one law, holds all events together, where each and all are inseparable and necessary parts of the one Reality.

If we dwell in eternity, why need we hurry in soul, whatever bodily hurry may be required? Why should we not dwell here in the everlasting now, instead of reaching off somewhere in thought, anticipating the future and death, as though there would ever be a break in the stream of life? If we, as souls, dwell in eternity, is not our life continuous? It surely cannot die if it enlarges into the infinite, eternal life, else it would not be life, but mere physical change. Even in physical disintegration there is no annihilation, not even the minutest particle is ever lost. Can we believe anything less of the soul? Must we not believe more; namely, that the aspiring consciousness and sense of individuality remain unbroken? If the great Father has a purpose with us, however infinitesimal as applied to you and me, it must be a part of his infinite life; and there is nothing to break its continuity.

In some of us has been born a desire to live forever. It is probable that we are no more responsible for that desire than for our deepest faith in God. In the supremest moments of human life it is he who stands by us, not we by our faith in him, and we would fain doubt him if we could; but we never quite persuade ourselves that he will fail to fulfil every deepest desire and justify all the conditions in which we have been placed, though it take forever. There are times when we seem to dwell in a region where all is good and wise and true; for we have momentary glimpses of the sublime wholeness of things, the sublime reason, the sublime end, a region where, if we have not all power, we at least have as much as we can make our own, and a faith that knows no doubt. Yet it is no credit to us that we have this faith, this belief in God. We did not originate it.

If I display goodness towards another, I partake of the nature of God in some degree. The love of God speaks through the heart of the mother. It must be a part of the infinite love, since we all belong to him; and, if we had any power wholly independent of him, all men, all things, would be independent of him. There would be no fundamental unity, no omnipresent, inclusive Reality, no universe as we know it. The life, the power, the goodness, the love, the groundwork of the universe, of men, and of the soul, must be the all-inclusive Self; and human nature, however individual in its history, must be at each moment in some measure dependent on the Universal. One's soul is not one's self alone. It is also God's emphasis of some phase of his own nature, the attention of God fixed on some object. One's unquenchable faith is ultimately God's unfailing love. We believe in him because he knows us, because he possesses us, you and me, and uses, has need of us, because he has made us aware of his presence. He loves us, and we trust him because we must. He has aroused interest in our minds in the deepest problems of life,— problems which it will take eternity to solve; and, if we long to solve them, we may thus know that we are so far immortal, because this interest is fundamentally the eternal purpose of God.

This realization of our oneness with the unthinkably great and eternal, which brings us just as near to it and makes us just as much part of it here and now in this present moment as though we were this great wholeness, and had lived from all time, is strengthened by considering our indebtedness to the world. Here we are in this beautiful, beautiful world. How wonderfully it is wrought! How systematically it has evolved, governed by exact laws and animated by unvarying forces! It is our own home. We can rely upon it and on that heaven-taught instinct which guides its creatures better than the combined wisdom of all mankind. What a delight to exist! What exceptional pleasures come to us at times among the mountains, by the winding streams, the peaceful valleys, the great ocean, inspiring awe alike in storm and calm, and ever suggestive of that Whole which unites us all! Days are continually recurring which stand out above many others because of some charming scene in nature, some impressive communion with the spirit of the woods or the hills, while the dreariest day in winter or the most barren landscape in nature will yield its gift of beauty if we seek it. The poet and the artist see all this, and live in a diviner world because they are watchful. But the beauty is there for us all, to inspire contentment if we need it, to reveal the good if we look for it, and do not let the habit of narrating and seeking only the bad control us, and to make us thankful and trustful when we consider its deep significance, its correspondence to the beauty of law and order, of need and supply in the inner life.

Then, too, the beauty of human character more than all else endears one to life, and gives one joy in existence. Two or three noble friends are all the world to some people. Where they are is home, and where they are is always happiness and contentment. One is constantly being touched by little acts of kindness and devotion. Sometimes in the country, even among a simple folk, one draws very near to the heart of humanity. One is moved beyond words, for nothing conceals the honest hearts that reach out to one in all their native feeling and sincerity. Such experiences have a wonderful effect upon the recipient when put beside the darker aspects of life,— with those undeniable evidences of wickedness which might otherwise almost persuade one that human life is corrupt to the core.

Omit these darker experiences we cannot in trying to cast our thought into some sort of system; but in daily life we are too inclined to dwell on them, especially to enlarge upon our own woes, to describe every detail, so that as a result our friends form harmful mental pictures of them. We are apt to contemplate these darker facts, and never get beyond them. We stay in gloomy surroundings, and then call the world ugly. It is well once in a while to pass in review all that should cause us joy and thankfulness, to ascend the mountain, whence we can look beyond the ugly spots and see their relation — and, after all, it is a beautiful one — to the great landscape beyond.

I do not speak alone as one who has stood on the mountain top, and thought the world beautiful, but as one who has suffered keenly and critically in the darksome vales below, who has met with the severest losses and suffered the deepest disappointments, and has had a most intense nature to overcome. Our poise is worth little if it fail to give strength and composure in any possible experience, and to be itself strengthened by the newest trial. The experiences and realizations suggested in this chapter prepare the way for the severer tests of actual life. If we habitually realize what it means to dwell with God, what the soul is, and how it is approaching completion, and keep the ideal of adjustment to life ever before us, pausing in silent receptivity whenever we become too intense, into the thought will steal the renewing and strengthening Power, which will prepare us for the day of sorrow and the hour of supreme suffering.

VIII.

SELF–HELP.

We have now considered the general attitude toward life whereby the vital truths of the Spirit may become concrete in daily experience. We have found that attitude to consist in the recognition of what man is as a progressive being, and in wise co-operation with the indwelling Life which resistlessly carries him forward to completion. There is a tendency, a guidance, in the soul of man which will lead him onward if he will listen for it. It will guide him in every detail of life, it will help him in every moment of trouble. It is with all men, it is used by all men; for otherwise they could not exist. But to the majority it is unknown and unrecognized, simply because they use it unconsciously; and to assure them that they can have such guidance seems to them the merest folly. To know it, and to distinguish between the merely personal thought or inclination and this diviner moving, is to live the higher life,—a life which seems infinitely better and happier the moment one learns to make this most helpful discrimination. To turn to it in times of doubt and trouble is to regain one's poise, to become adjusted to life, to gain the truest self-help.

Ordinarily, it is sufficient to hold this possibility in mind, and to maintain an ever-deepening consciousness of our life with the infinite Father. Contaminating influences cannot then touch us, fear will have no power over us, we shall respect this inner voice rather than the opinions of men, and escape a large proportion of the ills which neither the mind nor the flesh is heir to. This realization will add a meaning, a depth and beauty to life, which the reader who has not yet made it a factor in daily experience can hardly imagine. Simply to discover that so much depends on our mental attitude is of itself sufficient knowledge to work a wonderful change in the lives of those who ever bear this vital truth in mind; for, if we begin life afresh, with a determination to see only the good, the real meaning and spirit of things, it will be impossible for our old habits of thought, our fears and inherited notions about disease, to win their way into consciousness. The road to better health, to unhoped-for happiness and freedom, is open before us. The better health shall be ours if we have the will, for nothing can resist the power of thought: the body, our fixed directions of mind, and even our temperaments will yield when we learn how to use this marvellous power.

But there are experiences when we need something more than this general knowledge of how to take the deepest life just as it is; and, in order to make the application of the foregoing principles perfectly clear, so that the reader will not only know what to do in times of trouble and suffering, but how to help a fellow-sufferer, let us once more consider the actual process of change in mind and body.

In considering the qualities and composition of matter in Chapter III., we learned that the phenomenon of expansion and contraction is one of its most noticeable characteristics. Turning to the mental world, we found the same principle repeated; namely, that thoughts are harmful or healthful to the degree that they expand and contract the inner being. Fear, jealousy, anger, and all selfish or belittling emotions have a tendency to draw one into self, to shut in and restrict the activities, impeding the natural life and restorative power of the body, and developing a condition from which, if it be long maintained, nature can only free us by a violent reaction: whereas a pleasurable emotion, such as one feels when listening to a familiar melody or the strains of a great symphony, causes the whole individual to expand, and sends a thrill to the utmost extremities of the being.

There is a whole vocabulary of words in common use expressing the warmth and coldness of human beings. In fact, the two faculties of intellect and emotion, or head and heart, are often taken as types of these fundamental characteristics; and we speak of this church as cold and intellectual, that one as warm and spiritual,— so hard it is for one to combine the two.

Again, considering emotion alone, we speak of warm-heartedness. It seems to be out-going, expansive; and, if one give to another or do some act of kindness, that act has a tendency to repeat itself. The person is touched on whom the favor is conferred, and immediately feels a desire to reciprocate, or to show kindness to another. On the contrary, let the emotion be selfish, let the person decide to do a mean act, and there is an instant withdrawing, a self-contraction and narrowing of the soul. Happiness, joy, genuine pleasure, and self-denial are expansive emotions, and oftentimes wonderfully catching. With the one emotion comes self-forgetfulness and lack of restraint: with the other comes self-consciousness and painful awareness of sensation. Love is warm: selfishness is cold. Happiness expands: fear contracts.

Thus we might pass in review the whole category of human emotions; and, if we could trace their physical effect on the minuter portions of the body, we should probably discover that the molecules are either drawn together or thrown apart by each emotion. When the shock is too great, whether the emotion be one of joy or sorrow, death results. There is evidently, then, a state of equilibrium where, on the one side, the body is harmoniously open and free from restrictions, and where, on the other, the mind is also open or in repose.

This emotional effect, with its accompanying physical changes, may be further illustrated by the sudden and marvellous cures which have taken place in all ages, and are occurring to-day. It is a well-known fact that these wonderful cures usually occur either among people of strong faith or among ignorant and superstitious — in other words, highly emotional — people. The alleged cures performed through the agency of sacred relics, at holy shrines, at Lourdes, and other well-known wonder-working centres, are wrought almost wholly among strongly superstitious people, who are ready to accept certain beliefs with all the energy of their being.

It is a truism to-day to affirm that miracles are impossible. The whole fabric of nineteenth-century science rests on the knowledge that law is universal. If, then, such cures occur, — and they are too widely attested to doubt them, — they must take place in accordance with a certain principle. This principle is evidently the one already suggested; namely, that the bodily condition changes when the emotions are touched,— not only in sudden cures, but in all that constitutes the emotional life. And the reason is found in the existence of the subtle intermediary known as spiritual matter, which immediately responds to the slightest change of feeling, and translates it into the bodily condition.

The stronger the emotion, other things being equal, the more remarkable the effect or cure. Emotion of a certain sort — noticeably, expectant attention accompanied by implicit faith on the part of an invalid before a sacred relic — has a wonderfully expansive and liberating effect on the body. The whole thought is concentrated on what is about to occur; the individual is lifted above self by the emotional experience; and the physical forces are no longer hampered by fear, morbid awareness of sensation, and the thousand and one feelings which interfere with the natural restorative power of the body. The emotion frees, opens the body, so that the interpenetrating forces may once more circulate between the particles. Density is broken up. An expansion takes place; and a process of change which usually occupies many weeks or months is completed in a short time, resulting in the cure of many so-called incurable diseases.

Here, then, is an important fact underlying **the** entire process of cure and self-help: a change for the better results when the emotions are touched, when some thought or feeling penetrates to the centre, freeing the soul, and causing an expansion of the whole being. Something must quicken the activities and rouse the individual to new life. Bed-ridden invalids and lame people have been known to rush out of burning buildings, or forget themselves in their eagerness to rescue a person in danger, completely recovering their health through the sudden change of mind. In other cases, where the patient is selfish in disposition, the chief task is to find some way in which the person shall begin to live for other people, some interest which shall take the thought out of self, and thereby open the person to the healing power. Whatever be the method employed, — the use of physical remedies, prayer, foreign travel, — anything that arouses the confidence, the affection, the interest, or even the credulity of the sufferer, will produce the same result. On the other hand, any remedial means which fails to move or touch the soul is of little efficacy in effecting a cure. The problem, then, is to discover the method whereby the individual shall most quickly and easily be touched, so that **the healing** power shall have **full and immediate** access to the troubled soul.

But what causes the emotional change? Why is it that so many people who receive no benefit from medicine are cured by forgetting self and becoming absorbed in some benevolent work? If ignorant and superstitious people can be cured quickly because they are credulous, if cures of all kinds and among all classes largely depend on the faith or confidence put into the remedial means, is there not some deeper law which governs all cases, by the discovery of which the intelligent can be cured as quickly as the superstitious?

There can be but one answer to these questions. It is the thought, the mental attitude, the direction of mind, which governs the whole process. Before the sudden cure can result, there must be faith, expectant attention; and, if the person have implicit faith, the whole individual is governed by this one powerful direction of mind. The emotional experience unconsciously opens the soul to the Life or Spirit, which, like heat, enters into and expands the whole being, just as the warm sunlight penetrates the very fibre of the plant. It is the Spirit that performs the cure, not the personal thought or faith. The human part consists in becoming receptive, in withdrawing the consciousness from self and physical sensation, and becoming absorbed in the expected cure. The personal self, the fears and wrong thoughts, have stood in the way, and barred the door where the Spirit sought to enter. The new direction of thought changes all this, and makes way for the Spirit. It is a redirecting of the will; and in the wise use of the will, as we have seen, lies the greatest human power, while its misuse is the most potent cause of trouble.

Of all known forms of the one energy, then, thought is the most powerful, the most subtle, and, probably, the least understood. Used ignorantly, it brings us all our misery; used wisely, its power of developing health and happiness is limitless. It is essential to a just understanding of it, and to the knowledge of how to help one's self, that the reader bear in mind the central thought of each of the foregoing chapters. For we have learned that all power acts through something; and, in order to understand how the realization of the Spirit can break up an organic or chronic physical disease, so called, one must remember how such a disease is built up, and what the power behind thought really is.

We have seen that the inherited beliefs, the borrowed opinions and fears, the troublesome mental pictures, the description of symptoms made by doctors, and the whole thought process whereby a disease is made out of a disturbance which nature would have cured, had she been permitted, is impressed upon the spiritual matter, and then reflected in the body. All this must be changed — the mental attitude, the spiritual matter, and the physical body — by another and more powerful direction of mind, not of the personal self alone, but a realization which, consciously and intelligently, opens the individual to the healing power, to the same Power on a higher plane, which unconsciously heals the ignorant enthusiast at the shrine, but leaves him no wiser, because he has no understanding of it.

To many people it seems impossible that a person in a quiet attitude of mind can wield such power as this, and actually penetrate with the power of the Spirit to the very core of a diseased state and break it up, overcoming density and contraction in the muscles and tissues of the body which no physical remedies can affect. Yet this has been done repeatedly, and done, too, by those who knew precisely what they were doing and how they did it. The right use of this quiet, penetrating thought is a science, and every detail of this present analysis of the healing process is based on actual experience in performing just such cures.

The whole matter is simplified by remembering that the body is composed of minute particles, which may be driven farther apart by the attenuated substance which forms the connecting-link between thought and the physical state. Matter is not an inert mass: it is imbued with Life; and thought can penetrate to that resident Life, and become consciously connected with it. The power used by thought is greater than the power which binds the particles together; for it is the Spirit, and it can become the master, and is, in fact, constantly used by man in a masterful way, with scarcely a suspicion of the wonderful power he is wielding.

1. The first fact to note, then, is that the power of self-help is with us, like the air we breathe, awaiting our openness to it. In the moments of calm decision before referred to, when we master our fears or decide upon this better conduct in preference to that sinful act, we do not have to fix the decision in mind, and say, "This shall be so." The decision itself is an act of will, like the desire to move the arm, and is put into effect unconsciously to us. In the same way the ideal of adjustment to life, and the daily effort to gain one's poise, is effective in proportion to the clearness and strength of our thought and the confidence we put into it. The first essential is a healthier and wiser habit of thought, for the ideas that we have inherited and grown up with are narrow and cramping to the soul. It is our personal duty to have the right thought: our own organism will see that it is

executed. We do not need to fight the wrong thoughts, nor argue them away. It is enough for man to sow the new seed: nature will attend to its growth.

If the reader has carried out the suggestions of Chapter I., and tried to actualize these vital truths in daily life, or to realize the power of silent receptivity, it must already be clear that this is the most direct method of touching the inner centre. For, with the realization of the near presence of the immanent Spirit comes the conviction that it is competent, more competent than we, to minister to our truest and deepest need. A quieting influence, a sense of power and restfulness, steals upon us, removing all fear and doubt. The mere effort to become inwardly still is sufficient to awaken this sense of power, as though one were for the moment a magnetic centre toward which radiate streams of energy. And, if the reader has sought this silence in order to get relief from pain or some other uncomfortable sensation, there was doubtless a consciousness of pressure or activity in some part of the being, as though the resident power were trying to restore equilibrium. To unite in thought with this quickening power is, in general terms, the first step in the process of self-help by the silent method.

There is, obviously, no general rule which

should govern the thought process, because no two troubles and no two individuals are wholly alike. Sometimes one needs mental rousing; and the thought should be clear, strong, and decisive. Again, there should be little active thought; and, on general principles, the central thought of this volume — the power of silence — is at once the quickest and surest means of self-help. It is this power, and the attitude which invites it, which one should be conscious of, — not of the pain, the fatigue, or the depression from which one wishes to be free. This power or Spirit is shut out during trouble: there is resistance to it, and contraction in some part of the body. In order to overcome this resistance, one should open out inwardly, try to find the inward centre where the power is pressing through, or the centre of repose described in the foregoing chapter; and simply to search for it, and to rely upon this quickening power, is sufficient not only to draw the thought away from physical sensation, but to be immensely refreshed by the renewing presence. For, through this experience of receptivity — it is an experience rather than a process of thought — one becomes connected with a boundless reservoir of life and healing power. The healing process is, in fact, one form of receiving life. We do not originate life. We use it, we are animated by it; for it already

exists. Our individual life is a sharing of universal life. We possess it by living it; and to partake of it is the commonest yet the highest privilege of man.

In order to make this experience vivid and clear, let us compare the soul to the budding life which is trying to open its petals and expand into a beautiful flower. The soul has been through a round of experiences in ignorance of their meaning. It has come into rude contact with the world, and has sought to withdraw from the world's wickedness and misery. In thus withdrawing, it has shut into a narrow space the mental pictures and remembrances of the experiences that were repulsive to it. It has narrowed and cramped itself into this prison of its own selfhood, unaware that it was thereby shutting in experiences which must some time be opened out.

In the mean time the resident life, active in the soul, as in the bud, is trying to expand it, and to open it out into the sunlight of truth. This activity, being misunderstood, causes fear; and the soul, in ignorance, withdraws still more, cramping itself this time with the sanction of medical opinion.

Now, the thought of the one who understands this inner process penetrates to the centre where the imprisoned soul is trying to come forth, and gradually sets it free. For it is the nature of these deep realizations of the Spirit to cause expansion, to touch the soul; and the accompanying power is equal to overcoming any obstruction in its pathway. The expanding process may not always be pleasant, and oftentimes one feels restless and impatient to have it completed. It may require long and trustfully persistent effort to overcome a condition of long standing, for people do not easily yield their opinions and beliefs. At times it is only necessary to open one's self in silence for a few moments in order to take off the pressure and become wonderfully refreshed. Again, one has to try all methods,— to read a comforting book; to think of some friend, or a person in distress to whom one would like to be of service; to rouse one's self with a firm determination to rise above this troublesome difficulty, to push through it with a persistently positive thought, or do anything which shall quiet the inner centre and take one out of self.

But in all cases one should approach this experience with a quiet confidence that the resident power is fully equal to the occasion. It is here with the imprisoned soul. Help abounds. The Spirit awaits our co-operation. We belong to it. We need not fear: we only need be open to it, to let it come, to let it have us and heal us. It knows our needs, and is never absent from us. We are not so badly off as we seemed, nor is there any reason for worry or discouragement. Peace, peace! Let us be still, quiet, restful, and calm. Let us know and feel the eternal Presence which is here to restore us, and to calm the troubled waters with its soothing love and peace.

In due time, if this realization be repeated until one learns how to be still and receptive, one will surely become conscious of benefit and a quickening of the whole being. The mere form of words is nothing, and the above expressions are simply used in the hope that they may suggest the indescribable; for, once more, it is the Spirit which is the essential, the power behind the words, the experience which all must have in order to know its depth and value.

The ability to concentrate is the secret of self-help by this method of realization, and this is an art which each man learns in his own way. There must be a certain degree of self-possession, in order to hold the attention in a definite direction; and, if one have not yet developed this ability, it is well to approach this deeper realization by degrees, according to the method of Chapter VI. The process of silent help is, in fact, one of adjustment to the actual situation in the moment of trouble,—the realization that, individually, one has little power, even of the will, as compared with this higher Will, but that all that is demanded of the individual will is cooperation. God seems to need us as much as we need him. He asks thoughtful receptivity, and readiness to move with the deepest trend of the individual life. The whole experience is rather a wise directing of the will or attention, a realization rather than a process of active thought. The adjustment, the poise, the experience of silence, is a realization. The moment comes when the individual has nothing to say: the power of conscious thought becomes subordinated to a higher power, the Spirit. One cannot speak. One can only observe in silent wonder, in awe at the presence of such power, which the individual feels incompetent to control. This, in a word, is the highest healing, the most effective, the least personal, and the hardest to describe. One can only say: Here is the Life, the Love, the Spirit. I have dwelt with it for a season. Go thou to the fountain-head. It will speak to you, and be its own evidence.

This experience may be further described as a settling down into the present life. In all cases of illness there seems to be a withdrawing of the spiritual matter or body, as though the person were partially disconnected from the physical body for the time being. This is especially noticeable in cases of nervous shock and nervous strain,— that high-strung tendency which is made known through the voice, when the whole individual seems to be living in the top of the head. In such cases the effort should be to keep soul and body together and never let the one pull away from the other, to come down into the living present, to cease striving after ideals and dwelling in certain high-strung directions of thought, and never to invite any thought or experience which tends to take one away from wise and healthful adjustment to the eternal now. This is one of the quickest and most effective means of self-help,— this settling down, down, calmly and quietly, into one's deeper and larger self, into present usefulness and equanimity, where reside the greatest strength and the greatest power.

But sometimes one is unable to penetrate to the Source of all knowledge and to connect in thought with the Omnipresent Life. The Spirit seems far from one, and one feels wholly separate from it. In such cases it is better to make the realization more personal, just as one would rely on a friend who is ready to perform the slightest service and be a constant comfort during severe illness. One would naturally be drawn to such a friend in ties of close sympathy and trust. In moments of weakness and despair the friend would be one's better self, full of hope and cheer. It is in such times as this that our friends are nearest and dearest to us, that we open our souls to them and show what we really are. The mother's love, the friend's devotion, is thus the means of keeping many a soul in this present life when all other means have failed, — failed because they could not touch the soul, — whereas the communion of soul with soul through the truest affection opens the door to that higher Love which thus finds a willing object of its unfailing devotion.

Now, if in moments of trouble like these the reader will turn to the Spirit as to an intimate friend, help will surely come. The higher Self is still with one, but it is shut out. It is near, it is ready, like the friend, to help us, to guide, to strengthen, to advise, and to bestow comfort. One is momentarily disconnected with it and unaware of its promptings. One's personal self and activity stand in the way. The human will, fear, and all sorts of opinions have intruded, causing the Spirit to withdraw, and placing an obstacle in its pathway. To still the active personal self and let the real Self have us, to stand aside completely and let the Spirit return and fill the entire being, is, in a word, the secret of self-help in this as in all cases.

This is not easily done at first, and one is apt to force the wrong thoughts out of mind or try to reason them away. One often hears people say that they do not wish to think these wrong thoughts, but they cannot help it.

Suppose, for example, that one has a feeling of ill-will toward another, some unpleasant memory, or feels sensitive in regard to some word or act of a friend. Instead of trying to put away the unpleasant feeling by thinking about it, one should call the friend to mind and think of his or her good qualities, think of something pleasant, some good deed or some happy memory; for there is surely some good quality in every person. Very soon the unpleasant thought will disappear, and love and charity will take its place. It was not necessary to force it away, for one cannot hold both love and hatred at the same time. This exactly describes the way out of all difficulties, as simply and briefly as it can be told.

In endeavoring to find the good side of the person who has said the unkind word or acted impulsively, one soon becomes *en rapport* with the friend's soul, the real, the truest, and deepest person, who did not mean to act unkindly and who now regrets the unkindness. One's feeling of peace and forgiveness reaches the other soul, if the process be carried far enough to include both individuals in this quiet realization. One is lifted above the petty, belittling self to that higher plane of spiritual poise and restfulness. One has found one's own soul; and to find this, in moments of trouble, discouragement, sorrow, or sickness,— this is self-help.

Here is the inner kingdom of heaven,— a whole kingdom,— where dwells all Love, Wisdom, and Peace, whence we can draw power at our need and become readjusted to life. Here is where the permanent consciousness should abide. Here is the home of the greatest happiness and the truest health,— a happiness and a health which only ask our recognition in order to become fully and consciously ours in daily life, morally, intellectually, and physically, lending an unwordable joy to every moment of existence.

2. On the intellectual plane it is usually more difficult to find the inward centre and to realize the power of silence. The generally accepted opinions and education prevent one from getting into this higher state. Its own knowledge, its pride of intellect and assurance, make it difficult for the mind to surrender; and there is consequently much more resistance to be overcome. One is apt to forget that, so far as one has thought out the truth, that truth is universal: it is not the property of the individual alone. The very intellect whereby the truth was discov-

ered is a product or gift of the immanent Life, is an individualization of the larger Intellect,—just as life is a sharing of the immanent and bountiful Life in which we dwell, and of which we are not in any sense independent. Only the mere opinion or belief is purely personal; and it is usually just this personal element that stands in the way, some harmful or borrowed opinion, which prevents one from getting real wisdom. It is humility, willingness to learn, which opens one to the All-knowledge within; and, if one approach this experience in a purely intellectual attitude, one is not likely to feel the warmth of the Spirit, since everything depends on the receptivity or direction of mind.

In such cases, as, in fact, in all cases of trouble and suffering, the mind revolves in a channel that is too narrow. One needs to escape into a larger life, out of this narrow sphere of consciousness which has dwarfed and limited one's development. The very principles, the very habits, whereby one becomes devoted to a certain line of work to the exclusion of all others, causes the mind to flow in given channels, and never to pass beyond them. If this process be long continued, with but little rest or recreation, nature is sure to rebel, and to warn us that we must be wiser and broader in our thinking. And probably the surest way of getting out of ruts, and thereby avoiding the long list of troubles, ending in insanity, which result from the constant pursuit of one idea, is to realize our relation to the universal Life in which our own qualities of intellect and power inhere, and which demands of us all-round development, that we may come into full self-possession and complete soul-freedom. Rightly used, then, the intellect is the basis: it gives the only firm basis on which to rest the superstructure of the spiritual life.

3. On the physical plane the first essential is to explain to the sufferer that the healing power is present in the body, ready to restore all hurts, and that, if the person will keep still, like the animals, all will go well. On this plane one is in need of a wise counsellor to restore confidence and allay fear. The healing power meets with little or no resistance in the child; and, if medicine be kept away, and no disturbing influence or fear be allowed to interfere with the natural process, the mother can better fill this office than any one else. But here, as on all planes and in all cases, there is a grand opportunity for the wise physician, who, instead of making a diagnosis of the sick person, describing symptoms and giving medicine, shall quietly explain the healing process, and how one should become adjusted to it. In all cases of sickness the sufferer

needs comfort, needs to be told how to relax and take off the resistance; and in all finely organized people some understanding of the inner process already described is essential, in order to explain the keen and subtle sensations which would otherwise arouse the wildest fears. What a change would come to sick and suffering humanity if all physicians would adopt this helpful method, and cease all this disease-creating talk about symptoms,— if people would throw off all slavery to medical opinion! The best doctors would still have plenty to do, and there would still be need of the skilful surgeon. The world's suffering would be infinitely less, and we should then have an army of men striving to teach all-round self-development and good health.

4. In order to help those who are unable to get this inner help themselves, the first step is to find this same inner centre, and to realize for another the same peace and rest which is required for one's self. This should usually be accompanied by an audible explanation of the inner process, and how best to become adjusted to it. One person can help another only so far as one's own soul is developed in knowledge of and openness to the immanent Life. But during the quiet realization for another the same process will be caused in the other, if the person be receptive. One should therefore have confidence that help

will come to the recipient, — not through one's personal self, but through the quickening of this same Power within the receptive soul; and with this trust uppermost, and a deep desire to help the other person, a good result is sure to follow.

There is no effort to make a hypnotic suggestion in this experience of helping another, nor any attempt to transfer one's thought or feeling, but a realization of the needs and possibilities of the other soul. One cannot be in the presence of a person who is thus aware of the very presence and power of the Spirit without feeling the effect, consciously or unconsciously. Simply to meet a person who has spiritual repose is sufficient to cause a beneficial effect. To express it in the phraseology of Oriental thinkers, the same vibration is set up in the recipient; and there are those whose perception is so keen that they can detect the changes in vibration during a quiet sitting with a patient who is receiving help by the silent method.

It is only necessary for these intuitively acute people to become *en rapport* with another person in order to perceive at once how, to continue the same phraseology, that person is vibrating, or, more accurately, the surrounding atmosphere or spiritual matter which reveals the state of mind. If the agitation be intense, it must be stilled, not by entering into the agitation, but by keeping free from it, standing on the outside of it,— just as one would observe any change taking place in the outer world. The vibrations will gradually change, the agitation will cease, there will be a tendency on the part of the recipient to draw deep breaths, and finally a general feeling of quiet invigoration will displace the agitated condition both of mind and body. It may take many sittings to produce such a change as this; but the process is, in general terms, the same,— namely, a gradual quieting of all agitation by penetrating nearer and nearer the centre where the resident life meets resistance, and maintaining a quiet realization of the Power that is producing the cure.

5. But the best and most lasting self-help, after all, is that wiser habit of thought, that larger helpfulness, for which this whole volume pleads; for it is what we think and dwell upon habitually that moulds character and sheds its influence on the people about us. Our inquiry has taught us to look beneath matter to its underlying Reality, and behind physical sensation to the mind where it is perceived. We have found the origin of man, first, in the immanent Life of which he is a part, and of which he is an individual expression; and, secondly, in the world of mind, where his beliefs and impressions gather to form his superficial self. To know the

one Self from the other, to be adjusted to its resistless tendency, to obey it, to do nothing contrary to it, as far as one knows, is the highest righteousness, the most useful life, and the truest religion. Here is the one essential, the life that is most worthy of the man aware of his own origin and of his own duty.

There are many problems involved in an interpretation of life which we have neglected in this inquiry,— noticeably, those connected with the religious life and the great religious teachers. We have everywhere met an element that is incommunicable, that must be lived and practised in order to be known. There is much that can only be understood through patient investigation, much, too, that would well repay scientific investigation. Facts and possibilities are revealed through careful study of the inner process which throw a flood of light alike on the nature of mind and on the mystery of life. The thought is well-nigh overwhelmed by the scope and meaning of these inner experiences. It seems almost impossible even to suggest such insights and experiences to the general reader; for one must talk enigmatically at times, and rely on the reader's forbearance and willingness to test that which can only be proved through a similar experience. But it is everything to know that such possibilities exist, and to make a step toward their realization. It is enough at first to be turned in the right direction; to feel that help is for us, and only awaits our receptivity; to have some inkling of the great Power of silence. All else will come in due course if one have a deep desire for it. And, if we have considered the one essential, and begun to realize its deep meaning for ourselves and for our fellow-beings, the larger and more complex life of the outer world will be explained by the light and wisdom from within.

For, who shall limit the possibilities of the one whose life is centred in this spiritual consciousness, the one who knows the Real, and can tell it from the transient and illusive? Do we have more than the faintest glimmering of our own possibilities, — we who live beholden to matter, as if it were the all in all? Have we really begun to live, are we even half what we should be, whiffed about as we are by opinions and fears, at the mercy of other minds and of our own unconquered selves? Half the facts of life go to show that man is a product of matter, and his thoughts and feelings mere effects of a fateful outer cause. The other half show that he is a master, — a master in embryo, it may be, but a sharer of the only Life and the only Power by virtue of his individual will and his invincible power of thought. Life and all it brings him, ultimately, depends on his own wisdom and the intelligence he puts into it. He is weak and fearful, at the mercy of matter and passion, only as long as he lacks understanding. To know self and overcome it, to know the law and obey it,— this is the sum of righteousness; and all that duty demands of us at first is to make the start, to remember nature's law of growth, and persistently to keep the great end in view.

WORKS BY R. HEBER NEWTON,

RECTOR OF ALL SOULS' CHURCH, NEW YORK.

Womanhood. Lectures on Woman's Work in the World.

12mo, pp. 315 . . . . $1.25

"All earnest women, and candid, unselfish men, will read this series of chapters with warm gratitude to its author."—*The Nation.*

"No woman, young or old, can read these lectures without great profit. . . . The volume should find a place in every home where there is mother, wife, or daughter."—*Journal of Education.*

The Book of the Beginnings. A Study of Genesis with a general introduction to the Study of the Pentateuch.

16mo, pp. xv + 307, cloth, $1.00; paper . . 40 cents.

"These 'talks' will be acceptable to the general public, who wish to see on what grounds the critics base their conclusions respecting the Pentateuch."—*The Nation.*

The Right and Wrong Uses of the Bible.

16mo, pp. 264 . . . . 75 cents.

"It is impossible to read these sermons without high admiration of the author's courage, of his honesty, his reverential spirit, his wide and careful reading, and his true conservatism."—*American Literary Churchman.*

Philistinism. Plain Words concerning Certain Forms of Unbelief.

16mo, pp. ix + 322, cloth, $1.00; paper . . . 50 cents.

"We would commend these sermons to the thoughtful souls who want more light and stronger reasons for the old faiths."—*Chicago Inter-Ocean.*

Social Studies. 16mo, cloth, pp. 380 . . . . . $1.00

"Thoughtful, liberal, and tolerant in spirit, and marked by a tone of practical philanthropy."—*Boston Beacon.*

"Glowing, eloquent, engaging."—*Buffalo Express.*

"Should be scattered broadcast throughout the country."—*Providence Journal.*

Church and Creed. Three Sermons.

16mo, pp. xx + 212, cloth, 75 cents; paper, . . 40 cents.

"Written from a tender heart and with a deep Christian spirit. . . . Those who do not agree with the writer will do well to study his words."—*Public Opinion.*

"The author defends his position with a courage inspired by deep conscientious convictions, and with a manliness worthy of all praise."—*N. Y. Home Journal.*

Christian Science. The Truths of Spiritual Healing and their Contribution to the Growth of Orthodoxy. 16mo, pp. ix + 78, paper, 25 cents.

"We are free to say that this booklet of Dr. Newton's seems to be the very best thing that he has ever done, and we shall take the liberty to say that it is immensely better than his own description of it in the preface."—*Chicago Church Standard.*

G. P. PUTNAM'S SONS

NEW YORK
27 WEST TWENTY-THIRD ST.

LONDON
24 BEDFORD ST. STRAND.

Books by Horatio W. Dresser.

Methods and Problems of Spiritual Healing.
Pp. 101, 16mo. $1.00.

This valuable little volume contains the latest thought on the phenomena of metaphysical healing, and is the ripe result of many years of personal experience and observation.

The Power of Silence.

An Interpretation of Life in Its Relation to Health and Happiness. Ninth edition. Pp. 219, gilt top, 16mo. $1.25.

"The object of the book cannot be too highly commended. . . . It is really a charming essay, clear and exceedingly interesting. . . . It is a hearty, healthy, wholesome book; and it will do the conservative churchman, as well as the advanced thinker, a great service."—*New York Herald*.

The Perfect Whole.

An Essay on the Conduct and Meaning of Life. Third edition. Pp. 254, gilt top, 16mo. $1.25.

"'The Perfect Whole,' by Horatio W. Dresser, is a deeply religious essay upon the conduct and meaning of life, by one who has experienced the peace and joy that come from the belief that one Divine Spirit is working in all things and through all things. The volume lays no claim to originality of thought, but there is always original thought where there is such freshness and depth of feeling."—*The Outlook*, New York.

The Heart of It.

Compiled from "The Power of Silence" and "The Perfect Whole," by Helen Campbell and Katharine Westendorf, with a Preface by Helen Campbell. Contains the best passages from the two volumes, systematically arranged. Pp. 145, 16mo. 75 cents.

"These extracts have been made judiciously, and compose an anthology remarkable for the multitude of inspiring thoughts and for the beauty of their expression."—*Christian Register*, Boston, Mass.

Voices of Hope,

and Other Messages from the Hills. A Series of Essays on the Problem of Life, Optimism, and the Christ. Pp. 213, 16mo. $1.25.

"This new book will appeal to a very large circle of readers. It is in the direct line of all his former works—helpful, stimulating and comforting . . . no one can read it without feeling the better for it."—*Transcript*, Boston, Mass.

In Search of a Soul.

A Series of Essays in Interpretation of the Higher Nature of Man. Second Edition. Pp. 273, gilt top, 16mo. $1.25.

". . . Mr. Dresser's sane and helpful thoughts ought to be broad spread, for in such thinking we find something of that spiritual poise which marks the union of Heaven with our earth."—*The Outlook*.

Voices of Freedom

and Studies in the Philosophy of Individuality. Pp. 210, 16mo. $1.25.

This is the author's strongest, most philosophical book. It is broader, more fundemental than the previous volumes. It replies to criticisms, and contains advanced views and doctrines which are in some sense a departure from the teaching of the earlier volumes.

Living by the Spirit

Oblong 24°, 75 cents.

G. P. PUTNAM'S SONS, New York and London